HOW NOT
TO GO TO
WAR

Endorsements for *How Not To Go To War*

'There has to be a change in attitude on Foreign Policy and the UK's recent history of sending troops into battle. I have spent my life opposing these to see a Foreign Policy based on democracy, human rights and justice. And in the ministerial appointments, we may well be appointing in the future a Minister for Peace and Disarmament'.

Jeremy Corbyn MP, *Leader of the Labour Party in an interview with filmmaker Ken Loach*

'The proposal that there should be a Ministry of Peace within governments is not merely admirable, but, if implemented, would represent serious indication of actual intent. I'm happy to give my support to such a body whose responsibility would include being a consistent voice for nonviolent means of settling disputes.'

His Holiness the 14th Dalai Lama, *Nobel Peace Prize Laureate 1989*

'Vijay Mehta does not lose hope, does not give up the good fight for world peace, even as the world around us seems to be imploding. Of course, giving up should not be an option, as giving up in the face of the grave existential threats we face in almost every region of the world would be tantamount to suicide. So Vijay proposes that in countries and communities, in governments, private institutions and media, Peace Departments and Peace Centres be established to report on and promote peace. I fully agree, adding to the commendable efforts undertaken by thousands around the world in promoting peace, reconciliation, solidarity among peoples.'

José Ramos-Horta, *Nobel Peace Prize Winner 1996 and Former President of Timor-Leste*

'"There are no roads to peace; peace is the road," Mahatma Gandhi reminded us. A road oriented by principles and values. By justice, before all else. Peace is both a condition and a result, both seed and fruit. It is necessary to identify the causes of conflict to be able to prevent it. Avoiding conflict is the greatest victory.

'It is completely inadmissible that more than four billion dollars are invested daily into armament and military expenditures while thousands of human beings die from hunger and neglect. I believe that the present system is coming to an end and that, with the guidance of books such as *How Not To Go To War*, the "peoples" of today will be able to fulfil the immense responsibility assumed when they decided to "save the succeeding generations from the scourge of war". The historic transition from a culture of imposition, violence and war to a culture of encounter, dialogue, conciliation and peace, from force to word will initiate a new era.'
Federico Mayor Zaragoza, *Former Director-General of UNESCO and President of the Fundación Cultura de Paz, Spain*

'Vijay Mehta is an idealist: but he is a candid, hard-hitting idealist. He does not mince words. This book is controversial, but it is courageously challenging. It is certainly a work for our time. Whether we strongly agree or vehemently disagree with the arguments, it is important to read it. The stark truth it presents cannot be escaped.'
Lord Frank Judd, *Former Minister for Foreign and Commonwealth Office, UK*

'I welcome this contribution to the discussion on how we can secure peace in our increasingly perilous world. Ministries of Peace could play a key role in promoting conflict prevention and resolution.'
John McDonnell MP, *Shadow Chancellor of the Exchequer, UK*

'With inequality growing in almost every country in the world, it is more urgent now than ever before to ensure a fairer distribution of wealth and resources amongst people if the human race is to survive. In his timely book, Vijay Mehta catalogues the enormous waste of valuable money on the arms industry, designed not to keep us safer, but to make the giant military manufacturing corporations even richer. Unless we act now and turn our energies towards peace and life-enhancing products which are not environmentally destructive, we face an even greater risk of nuclear Armageddon than ever before in human history.

'Vijay's book is a vital read for everyone committed to peace instead of war and a more equal and compassionate human society.'

Fabian Hamilton MP, *Shadow Minister for Peace and Disarmament, UK*

'War is not inevitable. We need to create structures in our governments and societies which can avert conflict before it starts. The establishment of a Department for Peace is a powerful tool which provides programmes for education and support for community organizations to be more humane and caring.'

Dennis Kucinich, *American politician, who introduced the US Department of Peace Legislation to Congress in July 2001*

'We must wage peace with sophistication and commitment just as we now wage war.'

Marianne Williamson, *Author and Peace Activist on US Department of Peace Initiative*

'This book is just what is needed. How helpful it would be if we knew how to avoid war in our international relationships.'

Sir Mark Rylance, *Actor, Theatre Director and Playwright*

'My father, Vijay, has outlined a unique vision for world peace that would contribute greatly to fostering more equal, peaceful, passionate societies around the globe. I therefore endorse his pragmatic proposal for the establishment of a Department for Peace to be widely adopted by governments around the world.'

Renu Mehta, *Philanthropist and Founder, Fortune Forum Charity*

'There are many ways to peace and Departments of Peace are one of them, with a Minister of Peace in the cabinet. In this important book, Vijay Mehta spells out masterfully and in detail what a Department of Peace can do to bring us closer to peace. Get it, read it!'
Johan Galtung, *Founder, Transcend International*

'*How Not To Go To War*, with its call for institutions to parallel and hopefully replace institutions of war, takes such an obvious approach that it is surprising that so few people have explored it before. It is stating the obvious but still challenges the current culture, and especially the military-industrial complex. With all the military disasters of recent years, though, the time is surely right to rethink our very ideas about security, with Vijay Mehta's new book a welcome aid to that task.'
Paul Rogers, *Emeritus Professor of Peace Studies, University of Bradford, UK*

'Of Vijay Mehta's several full-of-merit books, *How Not To Go To War* is undoubtedly the most important one. We pay and prepare for war (under the guise of defence, deterrence, peace, security) but inevitably inflict and suffer endless war and violence. Mehta argues that a culture of war and violence pervades our societies and that its institutionalization urgently needs to be countered by that of peace and war prevention at all levels. The latter requires investment but Mehta shows that only a fraction of the overblown war budgets would bring enormous benefits. His book is an excellent elaboration of a key message of Ban Ki-moon, the former UN Secretary-General: "The world is over-armed and peace is under-funded." This book will be an eye-opener for many readers who will realize that there are untold promising avenues to lead to a world of peace and justice. The necessary funds to pave the way should come from governments (through public pressure) as well as from today's many philanthropists.
   'The world is in urgent need of successors to Alfred Nobel

and Andrew Carnegie who heavily invested into peace more than a century ago. I hope the author and publisher will succeed in putting the book into the hands of Bill and Melinda Gates and others who have joined them in The Giving Pledge campaign.'

Peter Van Den Dungen, *Author and Emeritus Professor, School for Social and International Studies, University of Bradford, UK*

'*How Not To Go To War* details revolutionary ideas to promote a culture of peace, nonviolence and conflict resolution to counter extremism, reduce violence and save some of the $14-trillion cost of violence and conflicts in our world. The UN's new Sustaining Peace Agenda focuses on the imperative to prevent "the outbreak, escalation, continuation and recurrence of conflict". It elevates the role of civil society, the private sector and regional organizations in sustaining peace. Vijay Mehta's ground-breaking and pragmatic ideas – including opening Peace Centres worldwide, encouraging governments to form Peace Departments and universities to develop peace studies – can help make this vision of sustaining peace a reality.'

Nadine B Hack, *CEO, beCause Global Consulting, Executive-in-Residence, IMD Business School, Switzerland*

'For the past 19 years, Peace One Day has been working towards establishing a day of global unity, a day of inter-cultural co-operation and a day when we stand together as one – 21 September, Peace Day. This day was unanimously adopted by all UN member states as a day of ceasefire and nonviolence. A Peace Ministry is a fantastic idea, one that would complete the circle within the governments of our world. I wish Vijay the very best of success in helping to manifest such a ministry.'

Jeremy Gilley, *Founder, Peace One Day*

'Vijay Mehta remains a relentless advocate of and activist for peace. His latest arguments to turn the war machinery of arms

production currently in operation into an institutionalized culture of peace testifies to his continued commitment.'
Henning Melber, *Director Emeritus of the Dag Hammarskjöld Foundation and Extraordinary Professor at the University of Pretoria and the University of the Free State, South Africa*

'I welcome Vijay Mehta's latest book, *How Not To Go To War*, as a timely, highly relevant and much-needed contribution to the urgent discussion on how to create a peaceful world in which peace has become extinct. His suggestion of having Peace Departments firmly embedded at the heart of government structures, supported by regional and local centres engaging citizens for peace activities, is radically imaginative. Implementing such concepts would undoubtedly have very beneficial consequences for world peace. By identifying necessary institutional structures for peace to counterbalance and hopefully prevail over the currently deeply entrenched institutions for war, Vijay Mehta has put the peace movement, opinion-formers and the wider public in debt.'
Reverend Brian Cooper, *Co-ordinator and Interfaith Secretary, Uniting for Peace Churches, Edinburgh, UK*

'Not in one man or in one generation can anything great be accomplished... Mankind, and life in general, is a succession of generations in which it is enough to nurture a spark from hand to hand, always in the hope that the flame will catch at last.'

Isaac Asimov, American author

'The greater the struggle, the more the satisfaction and joy in overcoming it.'

Shanti Mehta, Uniting for Peace supporter

HOW NOT TO GO TO WAR

**Establishing Departments for
Peace and Peace Centres Worldwide**

VIJAY MEHTA

How Not To Go To War
Establishing Departments for Peace and Peace Centres Worldwide

First published in 2019 by
Catapult
an imprint of New Internationalist Publications Ltd
The Old Music Hall
106-108 Cowley Road
Oxford OX4 1JE, UK
newint.org

Design and cover design: Juha Sorsa, New Internationalist

Printed by T J International Limited, Cornwall, UK
who hold environmental accreditation ISO 14001.

British Library Cataloguing-in-Publication Data
A catalogue record for this book is available from the British Library.

Library of Congress Cataloging-in-Publication Data.
A catalog record for this book is available from the Library of
Congress.

ISBN 978-1-78026-522-3
(ISBN ebook 978-1-78026-523-0)

Contents

The appendices include countries that have established
Departments for Peace: the Solomon Islands (2002),
Nepal (2007), Costa Rica (2009), South Sudan (2011),
Ethiopia (2018); as well as countries with initiatives that
aspire to have Departments for Peace: UK, US, Canada,
Italy and others. It also includes UN Resolutions and a
report on Peace and Disarmament.

Acknowledgements

This book is the culmination of my many years striving for peace, and my belief that the peace movement can and must establish a strong institutional base (Department for Peace) from which to grow. We need a peace-industrial complex, sustained by the same combination of public and private enterprise that keeps the military-industrial complex going, generation after generation.

The book required a great deal of research and reflection, and could not have been written without the assistance of friends, family and colleagues. Firstly, special thanks to James Brazier for excellent research and insight. I'm also indebted to Dan Raymond-Barker, Kelsi Farrington and Chris Brazier at New Internationalist Publications for guidance and advice on the editing, production and publicity of the book.

Secondly, I am grateful for the insights and passion of the grassroots peace community with whom I interact on the front lines of activism.

Thirdly, I must once again thank members of my family, Renu, Sanjay and Ajay, for their enthusiasm for my work, as well as my colleague Raceme who once again has been through the journey of yet another book.

Lastly, I thank my wife Shanti, whose name means 'Peace' in Hindi, for her love, wisdom and support.

Vijay Mehta
London, 2019

Introduction

The end-of-the-world scenario is palpable.

The threat of a nuclear Armageddon is now greater than it was during the Cold War. The United Nations (UN) institutions which kept the Soviet Union and NATO powers from each other's throats have become devalued and powerless, as global relations have degenerated into a new, frightening era of unilateralism by competing powers. Russia and NATO powers are entering a new frightening era of confrontation. From Afghanistan and the South China Sea to Israel and Palestine, Ukraine and Libya and Syria, the wielders of the world's military power no longer observe UN Resolutions and multilateral consensus.

The drastic deterioration in relations between Russian and NATO powers threatens an eventual collision which could prove catastrophic.

War has been institutionalized. Giant military industries, formed from thousands of companies, ensure that every old generation of war profiteers is replaced by a new one. Admirals, generals and senior defence officials demand that trillions of dollars be funnelled every year into the coffers of the arms trade. People whose careers depend on the cycle of arms and warfare insist that any break in funding is some kind of betrayal or national humiliation. Manipulated by vested interests, mainstream media justify increased military spending with spurious appeals to patriotism.

In 2018, the world spent an all-time high of $1.5 trillion on its uniformed fighters. That's equivalent to about $1,000 per family on the planet. Yet all these weapons have not made the world less violent. In 2015, violence cost the global economy some $14 trillion, a surge of 15 per cent from 2008. That number might seem high even before one considers the escalating inequality, famine, pollution, disease, collapse of public services, environmental damage and climate change that follow in the wake of war.

Institutions endure. They can outlast the people that create them. The question asked by this book is, how can peace be institutionalized? It finds that the institutions of war need to be matched by institutions of peace. For every Department of Defence, there needs to be a Department of Peace that allocates public resources to forestall violence and militarism by measures of pre-emptive conflict resolution rather than waiting for conflict to occur and then deploying violence against it.

Such Departments of Peace will be distinct from foreign and development ministries, compromised as they are by espionage, export-promotion and militarization of aid. By opening peace/social centres or franchises in each city, town and village, the peace movements can contain violence and foster a culture of nonviolence.

Newspapers need peace correspondents who champion peace just as many 'defence' reporters seem to champion war – drawing on the peace movements' wide ecosystem of thinkers, writers, artists and theorists. These aforementioned new peace centres would embrace these champions of peace.

Fundamental to all this is the pressing need for institutionalized peace – a network of self-sustaining peace centres and social enterprises and co-operatives, governmental peace departments and commentators who have peace as their core mission, in the same way that arms manufacturers and defence ministries institutionalize conflict.

Much as the Alco Hydro-Aeroplane Company, founded in 1912, evolved into today's Lockheed Martin, a $47-billion arms company bankrolled by taxpayers, this book shows how peace entrepreneurs can create profitable, lasting peace ventures and franchises that endure through generations, instead of fading with their founders. It describes how peace workers can find allies in the private sector, how conflict-reduction and nonviolence can be built into investment portfolios, and how 'non-profit' need not mean 'loss-making'.

The book shows how the establishment of 'Departments for Peace' and 'Peace Centres' worldwide will result in the taxpayer saving trillions of US dollars, which governments can utilize in job creation, healthcare, education and peace-building.

Only by institutionalizing peace at many levels of society can the peace movement become coherent and powerful enough to face down the many commercial and official networks that have a vested interest in armed violence. The time for action is now. There may not be a tomorrow to wait for.

This book is divided into two halves. The first deals with the world as it *could* be, with peace baked into our institutional framework in the same way that warfare is already budgeted for.

Chapter 1 – The Enemy Within explores the psychological underpinnings of military expenditure. Why do taxpayers consent to pay billions, if not trillions, of dollars to support military structures, even when their country faces no realistic threat of invasion and has not been attacked for centuries? Only by understanding this mindset can we hope to change it and obtain popular consent for deploying that wealth into more constructive directions.

Chapter 2 – Department for Peace explains why the time has come to establish Departments for Peace. These promise to be among the great institutional inventions of the 21st century, dragging the prevention of violence and conflict to the centre of the policy agenda. This chapter illustrates the broad but coherent set of responsibilities that would lie within a Department for Peace, and explains why other government ministries are inappropriate hosts for some of these. It shows how peace can be institutionalized within the public sector.

Chapter 3 – Making Peace Pay: Setting Up Social Business Enterprises in the 21st Century shows how peace can be further institutionalized within the private sector, by using the techniques of social enterprise and impact investing to place peace activism on a financially sustainable basis. For too long, the peace movement has made a virtue of shunning the financial, institutional and presentational strengths that keep the military-industrial complex in business. The time has come to harness the wealth of our society, and the access to power that it brings, to set in motion our peace-industrial complex through a network of enterprise and innovation. The chapter explains how, when combined with the Department for Peace, we can construct a peace-industrial complex, a network of private enterprise that profits from preventing conflict.

There are many ways that entrepreneurship can combine with activism, and this chapter offers a guide for peace activists who need a little inspiration for creating self-sustaining pro-peace businesses. Not everyone agrees on the underlying causes of conflict. There are psychological factors as to why humankind continues to valorise the machines and methods of mass violence, but identifying a single root cause of conflict is tricky. The strength of venture-based activism is that it allows a wide variety of approaches, rather than imposing a single top-down 'solution' with which many activists may disagree.

Chapter 4 – Peace Centres outlines how such spaces will work as 'civic centres' providing safe areas for children and adolescents avoiding the horrendous rate of street violence and murder. They will also address divisions in society in a more direct way, promoting a culture of peace – a multicultural environment in which conflicts can be resolved in a respectful and peaceful way. The Peace Centres would permit schools to specialize in peace education which can help end culture wars.

Chapter 5 – GDP for Peace is a chapter that advocates reform of national accounts so that they include only constructive economic activity, not destructive endeavours. Stated boldly, our notion of the economy, which is generally synonymous with aggregate gross domestic product (GDP), should not count the activities of arms manufacturers.

Chapter 6 – The Warmongers' Economy, however, urges caution when deploying conventional economic narratives. It shows that we need a new version of econometrics that excludes harmful economic activity, while doing more to reflect constructive works that do not always leave a cash footprint. It shows that peace entrepreneurs should have no qualms about asking billionaires to fund their projects. According to *The Sunday Times* Rich List 2018, there are 2,754 billionaires on the planet – more than at any other time in history.

The second half of the book offers a bleak appraisal of where the world stands today. It illustrates how the rules-based system that prevented the Cold War from ending in apocalypse has collapsed into a new era of unilateralism prosecuted by a 'Cult of the Strongman'. Around the world, major countries have fallen into the hands of men who believe themselves to be above the law of nations. Vladimir Putin in Russia; Donald Trump in the United States; Recep Tayyip Erdoğan in Turkey; Narendra Modi in India; Rodrigo Duterte in the Philippines; Xi Jinping in China; Benjamin Netanyahu in Israel and Jair Bolsonaro in Brazil.

These strongmen possess a new generation of weapons even more devastating than the last. The staggering resources devoted to arms development have resulted in devices that are about to overturn the existing balance of military power. Aircraft carriers and human armies will soon find themselves overwhelmed by swarms of mass-produced, miniaturized, autonomous drones. Artificial intelligence, facial recognition, mass surveillance, unmanned tanks, self-aiming sniper rifles and a great deal more that was once science-fiction have become science-fact. Can we trust the world's new strongmen leaders to use them wisely? These questions are posed by **Chapter 7 – Bullets That Think** and **Chapter 8 – A Clock Ticking to World War Three**.

Such men disdain what they see as the petty constraints of treaties. As the effects of climate change become tragically apparent in poorer parts of the world, Trump has shrugged off the US's obligations under the Paris Accord. Ecological destruction is displacing tens of millions of people, yet the response of the rich world is ever more callous, even though it is the lifestyles of the West that require so much energy and pollution to sustain. With more and more countries fighting over ever-scarcer resources, in the world's rush to emulate Westerners, the anger of the have-nots is rising. **Chapter 9 – The War on Nature** paints the consequences. The **Epilogue – Making it Happen** charts the way forward to a peaceful world.

Time is running out. Without action, there may not be a future to save. Let us act now, while we still can.

PART 1

THE WORLD AS
IT MIGHT BE –
A PEACE-INDUSTRIAL
COMPLEX

Chapter 1

The Enemy Within

'Pacifists ought to enter more deeply into the aesthetical and ethical point of view of their opponents.'
William James, *The Moral Equivalent of War,* 1906

What are the psychological imperatives that drive men to war?

War is a male pursuit; this much we know. The millennia of evidence on this point are quite clear. The inventors of war machines, the soldiers who serve, the generals who direct them and the civilian authorities who fund them are overwhelmingly men. This gendered nature of warfare should give us pause. It suggests that war is not simply a political choice, but the manifestation of some deep yearning in the male psyche. Even the eminent Prussian military theorist Carl von Clausewitz was mistaken when he said that war is but 'politics by other means'. On the contrary, for many men, war is an end unto itself.

Since our earliest civilizations, philosophers have sought to explain the existence of warfare. Often, their intent was to constrain those who would wage it. More than 2,000 years ago, the Roman statesman Cicero, a survivor of the civil war between Julius Caesar and his rival general Pompey, described warfare as the antithesis of civilized humanity, humanity being epitomized by reasoned discussion. Cicero viewed a rush to war as man debasing himself to the level of beasts and monsters.

Not all classical philosophers were so enlightened. Aristotle, writing two centuries before Cicero, extolled warfare as a process through which men could display their virtues. In his eyes, the four cardinal virtues were courage, temperance, justice and prudence, and the battlefield a theatre in which men could perform these virtues, or be exposed as lacking them. Even earlier than Aristotle was the Chinese philosopher Sun Tzu. Like Aristotle, he saw effective military commanders as the embodiment of cardinal virtues, and their relationship with their soldiers as patriarchal, like that of a father to beloved sons. He said that to kill in war, male soldiers had to be roused to anger, but the commander should not succumb to this emotion himself.

These ancient texts hint at a psychological basis for armed conflict, one bound up in cultural expectations of masculine behaviour. In his play *Henry IV, Part I*, William Shakespeare compared the refusal to serve as a soldier to the lack of virility supposedly induced by saltpetre, an ingredient in gunpowder. It was Samuel Johnson, the writer of the first English dictionary, who said in 1778:

> *'Every man thinks meanly of himself for not having been a soldier, or not having been at sea.'*

When his friend Thomas Boswell disputed the point, Johnson expanded upon it:

> *'No, sir; were Socrates and Charles the Twelfth of Sweden both present in any company, and Socrates to say, "Follow me, and hear a lecture on philosophy"; and Charles, laying his hand on his sword, to say, "Follow me, and dethrone the Czar"; a man would be ashamed to follow Socrates. Sir, the impression is universal; yet it is strange... the profession of soldiers and sailors has the dignity of danger. Mankind reverences those who have got over fear, which is so general a weakness.'*

The development of the academic discipline of psychology in the 19th century would contribute further insights into why taxpayers would tolerate so much of a nation's wealth being pitched into the hands of warmongers. One of the best contributions was offered by the US philosopher and psychologist William James, with his essay *The Moral Equivalent of War*. In it, James wrote:

'The military feelings are too deeply grounded to abdicate their place among our ideals until better substitutes are offered than the glory and shame that come to nations, as well as to individuals from the ups and downs of politics and the vicissitudes of trade.'

Like Aristotle and Sun Tzu, James identified a relationship between 'military feelings' and cultural ideals. The shared cultural memory of war was a 'sacred spiritual possession worth more than all the blood poured out' but, paradoxically, men vehemently argued against war nonetheless.

Yet the horrors of war were no deterrent – on the contrary, 'the horrors make the thrill'. To James, writing not long after the US Civil War, modern man had inherited the bloodthirsty love of war that marked Aristotle's ancient Greeks: 'War is the strong life; it is life *in extremis*.' This explained the fervour of the US media to fight with Spain, which the US duly did in 1898:

'In 1898, our people had read the word "war" in letters three inches high for three months in every newspaper. The pliant politician, [President William] McKinley, was swept away by their eagerness, and our squalid war with Spain became a reality.'

Like Cicero, James saw what he called the 'bestial side of military service', and he noted that more and more educated people were agreeing with him. The response of British and US generals and admirals, however, had been shrewd. They had clad themselves in the banner of 'peace', and shifted all the hostile motives to their enemies. In a sentence that rings eerily true to modern ears, James wrote:

'It may even reasonably be said that the intensely sharp preparation for war by the nations is the real war [–] permanent, unceasing [–] and that the battles are only a sort of public verification of the mastery gained during the "peace" interval.'

Modern man has a split nature on the subject of war, James perceived. Rationality and intellect tell him it must be avoided, but he has an emotional, 'romantic' revulsion at the idea of war as a transitory phenomenon that humanity must evolve beyond. This instinct rejects a peaceful world as a 'sheep's paradise':

> '[War's] "horrors" are a cheap price to pay for rescue from the only alternative supposed: of a world of clerks and teachers, of co-education and zo-ophily, of "consumers' leagues" and "associated charities", of industrialism unlimited, and feminism unabashed. No scorn, no hardness, no valour any more! Fie upon such a cattle yard of a planet!'

Although he saw himself as 'firmly in the anti-military party', James sympathized with this mentality, up to a point. He understood the concern that humankind's transition into a 'pleasure economy' would cause humanity to degenerate, without the harsh rigours of military action to prune the weak and preserve the strong. To James, this mentality explained why voters were willing to pay taxes to fund the military:

> '...taking human nature as a whole, its wars are its best protection against its weaker and more cowardly self, and that mankind cannot afford to adopt a peace economy.'

James believed that the failure of peace advocates to understand this mindset explained why they had failed to convert more militarists to their side. The cause of peace had failed to offer an alternative to war's 'disciplinary' function, but rather represented a leaden materialism that listed the financial costs of war in a way that had no appeal to the romanticism that fuelled the militaristic male imagination. As James put it:

> '...our socialistic peace-advocates all believe absolutely in this world's values; and instead of the fear of the Lord and the fear of the enemy, the only fear they reckon with is the fear of poverty if one be lazy... "Dogs, would you live forever?"

shouted Frederick the Great. "Yes," say our utopians, "let us live forever, and raise our level gradually".'

James's solution to the problem of war is one that is unlikely to muster enlightened support in the 21st century. Rather than declaring war on other countries, he suggested humankind should declare war 'against nature itself'. An army of young men should be dispatched to coal and iron mines, to fishing fleets, to road-building and tunnel-making, to foundries and stoke-holes, and to the frames of skyscrapers. There 'would our gilded youths be drafted off, according to their choice, to get the childishness knocked out of them, and to come back into society with healthier sympathies and soberer ideas'.

Whether such labour would indeed defeat the childish romanticism of war is debatable. Less so is the fact that James's vision is incompatible with the sustainable stewardship of the planet that must go hand in hand with its pacification. Nevertheless, the concept of a 'war on nature' must be carefully understood, because it explains another key psychological component of militarization and industrialization: the need for elites to provide adults, men in particular, with work. In many cases, this reflects a fear among elites that workless men pose a threat to the elites themselves.

Modern China is the Jamesian solution writ large. As the 2008 global financial crisis began to unfold, the ruling Communist Party of China readied harsh reprisals against jobless workers who were staging public protests. At the same time, the government unveiled a half-trillion-dollar stimulus programme designed to soak up the unemployed in public works to build roads, railways, irrigation networks and airports. In its practical purpose, China's stimulus very much resembled William James's 'war on nature'.

Today, the psychology of unemployment troubles elites worldwide, and not only in non-democracies such as the People's Republic of China. Even without a global economic crisis, the rapid march of automation threatens to make hundreds of millions of workers redundant. Confronted with this tsunami of psychological and financial insecurity, many governments are certain to see the military as a means of job creation for men and women who might otherwise subscribe to anti-system politics. The problem of mass militarization could be on its way to becoming more, rather than less, acute.

As I pointed out in my 2012 book *The Economics of Killing*, the US military already serves as an employer-of-last-resort for young Americans – particularly in the poorer southern states. According to the World Economic Forum, the US military is the world's largest employer.[1] It has 3.2 million people on its payroll. Given the romanticized public image of military service, and the ever-growing number of people whose employability is outmatched by machines, many other governments will be sorely tempted to expand the military payroll, by taxing the companies profiting from the automation.

The psychological benefits of work render this kind of mass mobilization more likely. The UK's Royal College of Psychiatrists warns that unemployment is heavily associated with physical and mental ill-health, depression and suicide.[2] It argues that having a job assists mental wellbeing by providing people with:

- social contacts and support
- a way of structuring and occupying time
- physical and mental activity
- an opportunity to develop and use skills
- social status
- a sense of identity and personal achievement
- money and other resources needed for material wellbeing.

Military service offers governments an easy solution for each one of these requirements:

- The military provides a readymade social hierarchy, which allows people of similar social and educational backgrounds to mix.

- It offers a highly structured system of time management and employee surveillance.
- It promotes physical fitness, reducing the economic costs of ill-health.
- In the West, at least, the military offers its recruits plentiful training opportunities.
- The public respect for the military offers its members social stature.
- Medals and a rank system offer a ladder of advancement and recognition.
- The military has a transparent and reliable system of wages.

In addition, military service offers opportunities for foreign travel and a sense of adventure. For better or worse, by providing such a structured and artificial career, it also removes much of the initiative required to navigate the unpredictability of civilian life. Veterans often find this a difficult transition, although a Pew Research Center study in 2011 indicated that much of this difficulty was linked to psychological traumas sustained in service-based conflict.[3]

Faced with a choice of declaring a China style 'war on nature' or merely expanding the military into national schemes of organized busywork, the temptation of many governments will be towards the latter. Already, this temptation explains much of the $1.7 trillion diverted into military expenditure by the world each year, and why that figure continues to grow. In most countries, few of these regular soldiers, sailors and air crew will ever be placed in physical sight of a real enemy combatant. Nowadays, most of the violence is delivered by drones, cruise missiles and small units of special forces.

Peace activists are familiar with the false argument that demilitarization will result in unemployment. After the Second World War, far from being unemployed, demobilized soldiers were quickly absorbed back into the civilian workforce, where they found plentiful opportunities. The

British military is a fraction of the size it was in 1945, but employment levels are high.

Nevertheless, with youth employment a pressing political concern, some European governments are reinstating the concept of 'national service'. When running for the presidency of France in 2018, Emmanuel Macron pledged to reinstate compulsory national service – 20 years after France had dispensed with it. Requiring younger workers to don a military uniform has the convenient side-effect of removing them from the unemployment register.

Macron cast the initiative as a means of restoring national cohesion and self-discipline to the youth; the kind of language that William James would have recognized and despaired of. Rhetoric aside, a more plausible explanation for Macron's policy was France's youth unemployment rate, which the European Union placed at 25 per cent as of 2016. In a country such as France, with a long history of revolution and urban rioting, this is a pressing security concern. National service is one avenue for mitigating it.

France was not alone in seeing national service as a kind of solution. In 2017 the famously liberal Scandinavian country of Sweden announced that it too was to re-introduce military conscription, having abolished it in 2010. Ostensibly, this was to combat the 'threat' posed by Russia in the Baltics, but it should be noted that Sweden's youth unemployment was running not far below France's at the time, at around 20 per cent. Women would be required to participate alongside men, as was the case in neighbouring Norway. Finland also has mandatory military service, as does Denmark.

Peace activists may wish to pause for a moment before condemning such policies. It should be noted that another country with compulsory military service is Switzerland, despite its long history of military neutrality and success in avoiding armed entanglements with its neighbours. Switzerland's armed forces are purely defensive, because the country recognises that the only legitimate use of force is

self-defence. In this regard, all citizens are expected to play a
role in defending Swiss borders in the highly unlikely event of
foreign aggression.

Contrast this situation with the UK, a European country that
eagerly participates in US-led wars, with the notable exception
of Vietnam. The UK abolished mandatory military service in
1963. Does this mean the British are more peaceful than the
Swiss? Not at all. A principal reason for Britain's abolition of
national service was because it was disliked by the military.
Commanders saw the mentoring and management of younger
citizens, many of them resistant to military discipline, as an
unwelcome distraction from their warfighting mission.

It might be the case, therefore, that the most effective means
of promoting peace is to redirect the military, and divert it
away from warfare into other, more constructive endeavours
like investment in eradicating poverty, mitigating climate
change and the establishment of Departments for Peace and
Conflict Resolution.

The regime changers

After the Cold War, for a brief period, it seemed as if the
world's armed forces would evolve in a more constructive
direction, deploying to peacekeeping missions, securing
supplies of food aid, participating in disaster relief, assisting as
emergency firefighters, and even as community workers. Alas,
this vision was not to survive the presidency of George W
Bush in the US, or the premiership of Tony Blair in the UK.

For those untutored in international law, it might seem
strange that the invasion of Iraq in 2003 was widely
condemned as an 'illegal war of aggression'. After all, aren't all
wars aggressive? What made this one any more so?

The answer lies in the Kellogg-Briand Pact of 1928. In their
2017 book *The Internationalists*, Oona Hathaway and Scott
Shapiro, two academics at Yale University, demonstrated
how this treaty transformed wars of aggression from acts of
lawful conquest into criminal endeavours. They distinguished

between what they called the Old World Order, and the New World Order produced by the treaty.

Under the Old World Order, the laws of war reflected the legal thinking of Hugo Grotius, a 16th-century Dutch thinker. In his eyes, might was right. A country that conquered its enemies was entitled to the fruits of its aggression, without legal debate over its ownership. The only proviso was that countries must offer some pretext for their warmongering. Pretexts were usually easy to find.

Kellogg-Briand changed this. It established that the only legitimate wars were those of self-defence. By implication, neutrality was no longer an option; countries could and indeed should refuse to trade with aggressors, because continuing to trade would legitimise their land-grabs. The integrity of national borders was sacrosanct. States that violated their neighbour's territory could expect the world to unite against them, economically or militarily. The Nuremberg trials of senior Nazis were made possible by the pact having made wars of aggression illegal.

This legal reality placed arms suppliers in a difficult position, particularly after the fall of the Soviet Union defused much of the hostility between Russia and the West. If the world was divided into sovereign states, and invasions were illegal, the market for military weapons would go into terminal decline. Countries no longer needed to worry about foreign aggressors surging over their borders, because the world would unite against any that did. Territorial disputes between neighbours were to be adjudicated by international tribunals, in a legal setting rather than on a battlefield.

Alas, a new ideology came to rescue the military-industrial complex. A new breed of 'liberal interventionists' decided that winning the Cold War wasn't enough. They believed that liberal democracy, having overcome Soviet communism, had earned the right to impose itself by force on countries where it was not present. It goes almost without saying that many of these 'liberals' had dense, deep and diverse professional exposures to the many giant corporations that constitute the US military-industrial complex. The consequences of their collective mentality for international law have been devastating.

Herein lies another psychological risk. When governments are spending hundreds of billions of dollars on maintaining their armed forces, politicians become gravely tempted to justify this outlay in a military context. Politically, it is difficult for them to admit that their armies have become giant job-creation schemes. Moreover, the quest of elected leaders for a 'legacy' by which they will be remembered in the history books, for good or ill, leads inexorably to them contemplating scenarios in which military power can be exerted.

Encouraging them in this regard are many voices whispering in their ears: generals seeking more resources for their troops, arms companies eager to test their latest creations on the battlefield, some colluding editors who know that war sells newspapers, extractive companies eager to secure new contracts, thrill-seeking journalists determined to forge a career in a conflict zone.

In 2018, the 100th anniversary of the First World War should have provided an opportunity for reflection and remembrance; for sober recollection of the horrifying loss of life that accompanied that conflict. World leaders gathered in France to pay their respects to the fallen, and to lay wreaths at monuments commemorating their sacrifice. Such events, at least in theory, are supposed to make war less popular, and militarism less viable.

In reality, remembrance has turned into the hero worship of armed fighters. 'When heroes of the First World War made playing fields out of battlefields' read one headline in *The Guardian*. 'India's "forgotten" heroes and the Great War,' read a headline in *The Times*. 'Trump let a little rain keep him from honoring America's fallen war heroes,' sniped *The Washington Post*. 'More than 120,000 crosses planted in Britain to remember fallen war heroes,' said China's official Xinhua news agency.

These are not populist tabloids, but highly regarded newspapers. The assumption that anyone who fought in a war is a 'hero' – provided they were on the winning side, of course – is ingrained in our society, even in the supposedly sophisticated media. Losers don't tend to receive the 'hero' treatment; the word is applied far more sparingly to US veterans of the war in Vietnam than it is to those who fought on the winning side of the two world wars.

The death in 2018 of Senator John McCain was a rare exception. In 1967 McCain had been dropping bombs on the Vietnamese from his aeroplane when it was shot down and he was taken prisoner. This series of events earned him the description 'war hero' from the US media – a description it never applied to the Vietnamese who endured being bombed from the sky and who eventually defeated the world's most lavishly funded military structure.

The idea that, by serving in a war, a person automatically becomes a hero is a very strange one. To mark the centenary of World War One, the director Peter Jackson released *They Shall Not Grow Old* – a documentary film that used colourized footage of the War and was narrated with recordings of soldiers who had served in it. These voices from beyond the grave were pragmatic about the absence of heroism involved, the silly ideas that animated the desire to enlist and the horrors they had witnessed on the battlefield.

But so long as 'remembrance' revolves around men wearing medals marching in front of awed crowds, it will be less an admonition against war and more an exhortation towards it. Our sanitized, militaristic approach to remembrance serves to place fighters on a pedestal, while relegating the suffering, bravery and loss of those who sought to save lives rather than taking them, the civilians who endured despite seeing their homes and livelihoods destroyed, and the tireless work of diplomats and peace activists who try to prevent wars, rather than participating in them.

Perhaps most insidious is the appeal to concepts of 'national greatness'. Nuclear weapons, aircraft carriers, fighter jets are all symbols of national virility and prestige and reasons to rally round the flag. In June 2017, Jeremy Corbyn, the leader of Britain's opposition Labour Party, looked nonplussed as he was quizzed time and again by a televised audience over his personal opposition to nuclear weapons – even though Corbyn clarified that Labour had no plans to relinquish Britain's eye-wateringly expensive Trident submarines.

Britain is by no means alone in this. Indeed, critics who dismiss such views as nostalgia for a lost empire, a common accusation levelled at older Britons, should examine their logic. A 60-year-old British person born in 1958 can have very little recollection of Britain's African empire, which disappeared in the 1960s, let alone that of the Indian subcontinent, which ended in the 1940s. India cannot be accused of colonial nostalgia, but it too invests heavily in military status symbols. The explanation is not nostalgia, imperial or otherwise, but rather the psychological pride that male voters in particular attach to military firepower.

It is possible, however, to learn from this model. For every institution that endorses, venerates and glamorizes militarism, and scaremongers the consequences of its absence, it is possible to build an equivalent institution that does the same for peace. Not only is it possible – it is essential.

---

1 Taylor, Henry, 2015, 'Who is the world's biggest employer?', World Economic Forum, 17 June 2 Royal College of Psychiatrists, 'Is work good for your mental health?', nin.tl/mentalhealth 3 Morin, Rich, 2011, 'The Difficult Transition from Military to Civilian Life', Pew Research Centre, 8 December, original URL: nin.tl/civilian-life

Chapter 2

Departments for Peace, and Why Every Country Should Have One

It is a curious fact that although almost every country has a Ministry of Defence, very few have a Department of Peace. In most cases, even the word 'defence' is a misnomer. To describe them accurately, they would be 'Ministries for War' or 'Departments of Attack', given their responsibility for maintaining and often promoting the use of offensive weapons against countries posing no immediate threat. These entities build war into the budgets and accounting practices of almost every country on earth.

The fact that the Pentagon describes itself as the 'Department of Defense' is almost, but not quite, Orwellian. In George Orwell's novel *1984*, it was the 'Ministry of Peace' that was devoted to maintaining the dystopian superpower of Oceania in a state of perpetual conflict with either Eurasia or Eastasia. Its motto was 'War is peace'. Perhaps the pervasive cultural influence of Orwell's work helps to explain why, in the real world, only five countries have ever created a Department or Ministry of Peace.

The first was the Solomon Islands, an archipelagic country north-east of Australia, which in 2002 created a Ministry for National Unity, Reconciliation and Peace after the conclusion of a pact to end violence between the islanders of Malaita and Guadalcanal. Then, in 2007, the Himalayan country of Nepal formed a Ministry of Peace and Reconstruction, marking the end of a decade-long civil war between the royalist army and Maoist insurgents. This had ended with victory for the latter, re-founding the Hindu kingdom as a secular republic.

In both instances the ministries were a response to internal conflict. The only country to establish such a department without having suffered recent trauma was Costa Rica in 2009. A Central American country which famously maintains no standing army and where the cause of peace has a high profile in political discourse, it changed the name of its justice ministry to the Ministry of Justice and Peace, shifting it to a new emphasis on conflict resolution.

In 2011, South Sudan created a Ministry of Peace, concluded a Comprehensive Peace Agreement (CPA) with the Sudan People's Liberation Movement/Army and signed the peace process to end the longest-running conflict in Africa.

Most recently, in October 2018, Ethiopia – a populous and increasing prosperous country in East Africa – created a Ministry of Peace to reduce internal violence, and also signed a peace accord with neighbouring Eritrea to end a 20-year-old war.

These five nations could soon be joined by a sixth, one much richer and more influential. Jeremy Corbyn, the leader of the opposition Labour Party in the UK, has said that if elected he will create a Department for Peace. He has already appointed a Shadow Minister for Peace and Disarmament, Fabian Hamilton, to lead it. A minister would be a very good start, but specifying his or her role is critical. To weave the role into the fabric of the British government, what begins as a minister must evolve into a ministry. Otherwise, it becomes all too easy for subsequent rightwing governments to casually dispense with the portfolio.

In October 2003 John McDonnell MP, now the Shadow Chancellor of the Exchequer, introduced a 10-minute rule bill in the UK Parliament for the establishment of a Ministry for Peace, with cross-party support. The bill was supported by Elfyn Llwyd, Alex Salmond, John Randall, Dr Rudi Vis, Alan Simpson, Jeremy Corbyn, Alice Mahon, Kelvin Hopkins and Diana Basterfield. It was passed unopposed but fell for lack of parliamentary time. The bill emphasized the need to create infrastructures for peace based on peace-building and conflict transformation efforts. A Department for Peace will focus on developing a society based on direct, structural and cultural nonviolence and provide an alternative approach to security in Britain and around the world.

As a longstanding member of the peace movement, Corbyn's approach would mark a shift away from the bellicose approach of previous British governments, which over the past two decades have used overt or covert armed force in Afghanistan, Iraq, Libya, Mali, Sierra Leone, Somalia, Syria and the former Yugoslavia.

Were the UK to lead on the creation of such a Department for Peace, it is likely that many other countries would follow suit. One obstacle to the creation of new ministries, particularly in very poor countries, is that ministerial portfolios are so often a source of political patronage at best, and grand corruption at worst. Large cabinets are generally associated with political unwieldiness, corruption and weak decision-making. Pioneering new portfolios are often viewed with suspicion by foreign diplomats and advisers.

But were a permanent member of the UN Security Council to form such a ministry, a precedent would be set that would overcome many of these criticisms. This would be all the more the case if this Ministry were afforded real, discrete powers. It could become a template for such ministries elsewhere. And fortunately, there are many clear functions that should rightfully fall within the Ministry's portfolio.

Some of the functions of the Department for Peace would include: support and promotion for peace; diplomacy; international law; general and complete disarmament, including nuclear and conventional weapons; nonviolent soft power approaches to security; and diversification of the arms trade and armaments.

Dr Tim Street, in his report produced for Conscience on the Minister for Peace and Disarmament (MPD), outlined

10 potential strengths of the role of Minister for Peace and Disarmament. He also pointed out six concerns and criticisms regarding the Minister for Peace and Disarmament proposal.

The potential strengths of the role are:

a) Institutionalizing a school for peace, diplomacy and international law
b) Contributing to peace and disarmament education
c) Promoting alternative approaches to security such as non-offensive defence
d) Linking up peace and disarmament with environmental and social justice
e) Developing the UK's conflict resolution and peace-building work
f) Realizing arms conversion and defence diversification / reducing military spending
g) Advancing nuclear disarmament and the nuclear ban treaty
h) Ensuring the participation of women and a gender perspective policymaking
i) Engaging with civil society at home and abroad
j) Diverting tax contributions to support nonviolent approaches to security.

The concerns and criticisms of the role are:

a) The danger of the MPD becoming merely 'window dressing'
b) Lack of an international partner or disarmament workplan / tensions with Russia
c) Previous problems with posts similar to MPD
d) Duplicating existing work of other departments / money better spent elsewhere
e) Problematic 'Peace and Disarmament' title
f) Lack of public support and awareness / media opposition.

The role must not be too narrow or weak.

A short history of Peace Departments

The concept of a Department or Ministry of Peace is not a new one. In 1969 Frederick L Schuman, a political science professor in the US, published a pamphlet entitled 'Why a Department of Peace?'. Schuman noted that even as early as the late 1960s, the idea had been 'proposed many times by many thoughtful citizens and lawmakers'.

For instance, he recalled how in 1943 Alexander Wiley, a Republican senator from Wisconsin, made the following plea to President Franklin Roosevelt:

> *'I spoke on the floor in relation to a Department of Peace. I stated at that time that I craved for my government the distinction of being the first government on earth to establish a Secretary of Peace. The establishment of such a secretariat would be heralded throughout the world.'*

Wiley was prosecuting much the same agenda as Senator Matthew Neely, a Democrat from West Virginia, who before the outbreak of the Second World War had repeatedly presented a bill to establish a department of peace in Washington DC.

The genesis of the idea was much older even than that. One hundred and fifty years earlier two men, the African American Benjamin Banneker and his white friend Dr Benjamin Rush, a physician from Philadelphia, wrote an essay calling for 'an office for promoting and preserving perpetual peace in our country'. Published in 1793, it noted the United States' ongoing war against indigenous Americans and commented:

> *'It is hoped that no objection will be made to the establishment of such an office, while we are engaged in a war with the Indians [sic], for as the War Office of the United States was established in a time of peace, it is equally reasonable that a Peace Office should be established at time of war...'*

Banneker was famous for constructing the first clock to be made in the 'New World', and for a widely circulated farmers' almanac he wrote and published himself. His words against war were heard enthusiastically by Thomas Jefferson, the principal author of the US Declaration of Independence, who had commissioned Banneker to help design the federal capital Washington DC. Despite Jefferson's warmth, however, a Department of Peace was not forthcoming.

Schuman argued that because conflicts of interests between nations were inevitable, a Department of Peace would be charged with pre-empting these conflicts and searching for peaceful resolutions to them. This would defuse the crises besetting humanity before they exploded into violence. Schuman, of course, was writing only seven years after the Cuban Missile Crisis which had brought humankind to the brink of nuclear Armageddon.

After the Second World War, the campaign for a US Department of Peace intensified. Schuman notes that between 1955 and 1968, no fewer than 85 bills were introduced in Congress calling for the creation of a Peace Department. Unusually, there was little visible partisan divide; the bills drew support from Republicans and Democrats, unions and business owners, and from across the religious spectrum. Indeed, more curious was the fact that the bills failed despite any clear and visible organized opposition to them. Schuman attributed this to apathy on the part of the electorate.

There were some gains, eventually. In 1984 Congress established a US Institute of Peace (USIP), under President Ronald Reagan, which today is housed in one of Washington DC's most imposing buildings overlooking the Lincoln Memorial. USIP trains US diplomats and military officers on how to avert conflicts before they begin, as well as training mediators from conflict-prone countries. The institute currently has staff in 13 countries and is active in 51. However, its history is a valuable lesson for anyone seeking a Department of Peace, because it demonstrates many of the pitfalls that such a department must somehow avoid.

Although designed to be politically independent, USIP has

been accused of partisan bias since its inception, with the original Reagan appointees to its board of directors attracting the disapproval of leftwing Democrats. Peace activists question why the board of USIP must always include the US Secretary of Defense and the president of the National Defense University, as well as, currently, men such as Stephen Hadley, a former foreign policy adviser to the notably un-peaceful presidency of George W Bush.[1] It has even been accused of promoting nonviolent means of aggression, such as trade sanctions and psychological warfare. Critics have dismissed USIP's research, training programmes and local partnerships as ineffectual at best, 'jobs for the boys' at worst, and, at the very worst, as covert operations for the military.

From the other end of the political spectrum, its rightwing detractors accuse USIP of failing to prevent war and thus being a waste of money. Although many metrics show that the incidence of armed conflict has declined since the institute's foundation, the relationship between cause and effect is too complex for such critics to grant USIP any credit.

In 2017 the institute was targeted for de-funding by President Donald Trump's administration, which wanted to cut civilian expenditure and funnel it instead into the military. USIP, however, had allies and logic on its side. At about $35 million, its annual budget is tiny – equating to less than half the cost of a single F-35 fighter jet. It even funds some of its own budget by selling books and undertaking other forms of fundraising.

Moreover, USIP can point to solid evidence that it has pre-empted or peacefully resolved violent situations. In 2015, for instance, USIP-trained Iraqi mediators were instrumental in striking a truce between Sunni and Shi'a militants in Tikrit, Iraq.[2] They have recorded similar successes elsewhere in Iraq and worldwide. After the Dayton Accords were signed in 1995 to end the war in Yugoslavia, USIP spent a decade building communications channels between former enemies and combatants to ensure that peace took hold.[3]

These facts explain why USIP has survived for more than

three decades, despite criticism from both Left and Right.
Nevertheless, its experience provides valuable lessons for
any Department of Peace. The department's work must be
shown to be both effective and cost-effective if it is to survive
bipartisan scrutiny. How can this be achieved?

The need for diplomacy between countries is already well
understood. By maintaining channels of communication,
understanding each other's culture and ideology, promoting
cultural exchanges, monitoring behaviour and negotiating on
issues of discord before they result in violence, international
diplomacy is recognized as an essential function of every
single government on the planet.

Given this consensus, it is strange that there is much less
emphasis on the need for diplomacy *within* countries. With
every passing week we see how animosity between groups can
escalate into deadly acts of violence. The first responsibility
of a Department for Peace must be to establish the internal
diplomatic channels to forestall such bloodshed.

The sociologist Émile Durkheim suggested that social
malaise manifests itself as particular forms of crime. If this is
so, then inter-group violence can be viewed as symptomatic of
wider sicknesses in society, but their nature is not always clear.
In 2011 experts looked on as rioters tore London apart in an
orgy of looting, robbery and vandalism that erupted without
warning or any clear motive. Five people died, three thousand
were arrested and £200 million-worth of damage was
recorded. The response of the media was perplexed. As usual,
most interpreted the events through their own ideological
prism. A Department of Peace is needed to counter that sort of
confirmation- and information-bias; to conduct a kind of social
post-mortem. Only by carefully understanding the mindset
of those who perpetrate such violence, and the grievances
that fuel them, can an accurate picture of cause and effect be
formed. This diagnostic function would be one that fell to our
Department for Peace.

Peace and reconciliation at home should no longer be the

province only of countries that are emerging from outright insurgency or civil war. Rather, it must become an ongoing process in every country to promote discourse between groups that display mutual misunderstanding and suspicion. This is true not only between religious groups and secular society, but also between ethnic minorities and the police, between old and young, rich and poor, urban and rural, capital cities and outlying regions.

At worst, friction between groups can exhibit itself as the kind of terrorism associated with the so-called Islamic State, whose four attacks in the first half of 2017 claimed the lives of 35 people in the UK and left dozens more injured. Yet Islamist radicalism is only one example of a wide array of traumatic and violent incidents resulting from a shortfall in mutual respect and understanding between groups. Such social divisions and their violent consequences are most vividly displayed in the US.

In June 2017, a senior congressman from the Republican Party, Steve Scalise, was attending a charity baseball game when he was shot and seriously injured by a radicalized leftwing activist. Two months later a 32-year-old woman was killed in Charlottesville, Virginia, when a white supremacist rammed his car into a group of anti-fascist activists counter-protesting against far-right demonstrations. The latter group had gathered to prevent the local authorities removing a statue of Robert E Lee, a Civil War general whose portrayal was deemed by leftwing activists as a symbol of racial oppression.

That the southern states of the US should maintain monuments to what was the defeated side in the Civil War is highly unusual, but not unprecedented. A statue of Oliver Cromwell can be seen outside London's Palace of Westminster, even though his attempt to oust the monarchy ultimately failed. But in a world where traditional concepts of group identity are under constant review and revision, it is easy to see how such monuments can be the places at which destabilizing psychological and political crosscurrents converge.

Digital divide

Political divides have always existed, but the internet has
placed a premium on commentary that presents current affairs
in the most inflammatory and binary terms, and that tramples
cherished notions simply to shout above the noise generated by
the hyper-competitive world of free online media. Following
the near-fatal shooting of another member of congress, Gabby
Giffords, in 2011, President Barack Obama issued a call to 'help
usher in more civility in our public discourse'. Sadly, in the
intervening years, the situation has only deteriorated.

The word 'clickbait' is a neologism. It refers to the title of a
webpage designed to attract as many unique page impressions
as possible, irrespective of other considerations. These links,
scattered on newspaper websites, offer 'One Weird Trick to
Beat Cancer' or '8 Ways to Make Him Notice You'. They drive
traffic to websites, which increases their appeal to advertisers
and thus expands their revenue streams. Media organizations
use clickbait to attract viewers, and the smaller and more
'insurgent' they are, the more attention-seeking their clickbait
must be.

Clickbait is one of the manifold ways in which the media
has changed in the internet era. One principle has remained
the same, however. Alarming news sells. A giant study of
the media in 2007 found that consumers of news remain far
more interested in bad news than in positive developments.[4]
Newspapers and their online analogues are now competing
more fiercely than ever before to deliver bad news. Clickbait in
the news media is rife, driving headlines such as 'Birth control
makes women unattractive and crazy' (Breitbart News) and
'Earth to Trump – f**k you!' (*Berliner Kurier*).

Hyper-partisan websites that employ bloggers rather
than trained journalists, and which report only news stories
that comport with their worldview, have found that they
can achieve huge audiences via careful use of social-media
platforms such as Facebook, Twitter and Reddit. Mixing facts
with aggressive commentary and sometimes outright fiction,

these outlets harden political and social divisions by depicting their political opponents not only as misguided, but as actively malignant and conspiratorial. This editorial stance attracts more readers than one designed to forge consensus.

Articles that require dealing with complexity – challenging the assumptions of those on all sides of the political spectrum – are much harder to publicize in the new media environment. A psychological theory known as selective exposure, also known as confirmation bias, suggests that many individuals actively seek out information that confirms their existing beliefs, and shun news that challenges them. In the era of online news, with a plethora of news outlets catering to narrow ideological viewpoints, it has never been easier for such groupthink to thrive. In the UK, for instance, recent additions to the media scene include *The National*, which caters to supporters of Scotland's independence, and *The New European*, which serves British people opposed to their country's exit from the European Union.

Into this mix, according to Western governments, have waded the intelligence services of Russia. In a speech in November 2017, British Prime Minister Theresa May warned Russia that her intelligence agencies were aware of their attempts to sow discord. According to US sources, Russian-based Facebook accounts have organized protests on US soil on a number of social issues, particularly around the 2016 presidential election. If true, it does not appear that Russia is promoting any particular ideology, but rather just fermenting street-level turmoil between groups of angry people. According to the chairman of the Senate Intelligence Committee, Senator Richard Burr, Russian *agents provocateurs* organized a protest at the Islamic Da'wah Center in Houston, Texas, in May 2016 – and a counter-protest at the same time and place.[5] Burr said this cost Russia about $200 to orchestrate.

If it is so cheap and easy for foreign governments to sow social discord, then logic dictates that at least as many resources should be dedicated to countering this sort of activity.

A Department for Peace can take the lead in identifying groups whose differences threaten to spill over into aggression, and proactively seek to reconcile their differences with community relations programmes, de-radicalization efforts, prison visits, public diplomacy and international outreach.

Racial tensions must be addressed urgently. On 17 June 2015 a white supremacist named Dylan Roof murdered nine African Americans at a church in Charleston, South Carolina, including a state senator. In his confession, Roof said he had hoped to ignite a race war or bring back racial segregation. Roof would also claim to be a sociopath and, although he was found mentally fit to stand trial, the ease with which deranged individuals can obtain firearms in the US is yet another factor of violent radicalization.

A Department for Peace would control the de-radicalization programmes required to prevent political or racial anger from boiling over into something even worse. At the moment, de-radicalization programmes are led by the same departments and ministries responsible for policing, immigration, espionage and counter-terrorism. These linkages run the risk of instilling immediate resistance to de-radicalization efforts by appearing to pre-criminalize and thereby alienate the very people they are attempting to reconcile to mainstream society.

In December 2017 the UK's parliamentary Defence and Intelligence Committee released its annual report in which it noted that the government's 'Prevent' anti-terrorism programme is:

'...having a significant marginalizing effect, in that it places a target on British Muslims and the institutions with which they associate. There is also a sense amongst some parts of the Muslim community that Prevent is about police snooping, and co-operation with the programme can be associated with "snitching". Therefore, some argue that the policy is in fact counterproductive.'

Moreover, the importance placed on de-radicalizing Muslims

in the context of Western invasions of and airstrikes against Muslim-majority countries such as Iraq, Afghanistan, Libya and Syria has diverted attention from the need to de-radicalize other elements of society. It runs the risk of appearing to victimize Muslim minorities, thus spurring rather than preventing their radicalization.

As the above examples demonstrate, de-radicalization is every bit as important in the context of racial and political divisions, which are themselves often underpinned by economic inequality, social exclusion and cultural difference. Re-homing the process within a Department for Peace would help to correct the popular misconception that de-radicalization is exclusively aimed at Muslims, or that it is a policing tactic. This would be even more the case if the process were expanded to cover political and labour divisions.

In the UK, the Advisory, Conciliation and Arbitration Service (Acas) is a non-departmental public body of the government. Acas and similar dispute-resolution agencies could fall under the budget of the Department for Peace. As well as mediating between disputants, Acas and similar bodies in other countries could potentially lend their expertise to businesses on how to avert disputes before breaking ground on new projects, through consultation with the local community.

An example of where this approach might have value was the Dakota Access Pipeline, a piece of oil infrastructure that led to protests in 2016 between Native Americans on one side, who were joined by many other activists, and the police, army and oil company on the other. Although the tribes' objections to the project, which threatened to contaminate local water supplies and cut through a Sioux burial ground, could easily have been anticipated, they were not, leading to months of delays and a public-relations disaster.

Such advice could be even more valuable for Western businesses investing in poor countries. Departments of Peace in such countries could assist foreign investors in ensuring that their corporate social responsibility programmes and the scope and nature of their activities are aligned with public sentiment. For instance, if Coca-Cola were to build a bottling plant in a water-stressed African country, the country's Department of Peace could advise its executives beforehand on how to compensate local farmers whose irrigation is threatened by the plant's water usage. Investment projects with a sizeable environmental footprint would particularly benefit from this kind of professional, indigenous advice.

This is particularly crucial in the context of global warming. In early 2018 Coca-Cola's distributor in Cape Town, South Africa, found itself confronted by a coalition of 70 civil-society organizations (CSOs) which called on the company to halve its production over three months or distribute water for free to the worst-affected areas in Western Cape – an area experiencing its worst-ever water crisis. On that occasion the company involved dealt with the issue responsibly, pledging to provide access to the Newlands water spring and to distribute bottled water in the event of 'day zero' – the date at which the Cape Town's water reserves would reach below 13.5 per cent and authorities would go into crisis mode. The near certainty of such future confrontations, and the likelihood that companies will not always be able to accommodate the demands of protesters, makes Departments of Peace all the more essential.

Peace beyond borders

Overseas, Departments for Peace would be the natural home of outreach institutions devoted to cultural exchange such as the Peace Corps, the Confucius Institute, the British Council and the Goethe-Institut. They could take responsibility for government-funded state media outlets such as the Voice of America, Russia Today and the BBC World Service, recasting the activities of such broadcasters as being in the interests of humanity in general rather than as a tool of foreign policy or propaganda. Set within the Department for Peace, their journalism could be a much-needed antidote to the sensationalism, bias and unreliability of free online media.

It is a sad truth that whereas most news organizations employ war correspondents, they tend not to employ peace correspondents. War correspondents have a professional interest in 'talking up' the prospects for military engagements, to justify their own existence to their editors. Pro-peace news services would seek to counter not only 'fake news' but also offset the corrosive 'if it bleeds it leads' culture that has long characterized commercial news coverage.

Instead, the nationalized news agencies would offer even-handed, authoritative information. In this regard, they would be no more 'propaganda' than the swathes of news websites dedicated to sowing social discord in order to attract readers and advertising revenue, and certainly no more so than any activity by foreign governments designed to destabilize the political order.

The Department for Peace would work closely with peace-promoting international organizations such as UNESCO, as well as offering its dispute-resolution specialists as mediators in conflict zones everywhere from the Palestinian Territories to South Sudan. While the obstacles to achieving peace in such areas are high, so too are the potential rewards in terms of a country's 'soft power' and international reputation.

Further strengthening this 'soft power', the Department of Peace would also work towards unilateral and multilateral nuclear disarmament, as well as monitoring elections in emerging democracies, and helping to establish Truth and Reconciliation Commissions for countries that have recently emerged from conflict.

Peace Departments would work closely with academia, particularly those universities that teach diplomacy, international relations and conflict resolution. They would offer grants to researchers to devise specific mechanisms and approaches to real-world conflicts that require resolution, while ensuring that the current academic consensus on the causes and risks of war was made clear at the highest levels of government. Often, politicians represent academic thinking as it existed during their own university studies. In other words, it is decades out of date.

Importantly, the Minister for Peace would seek to counter narratives designed to persuade the general public in favour of overseas invasions and Cold War-style thinking that pits one 'superpower' against another. One of the primary reasons for the current animosity between the West and Russia is the vast number of officials, generals and spies on both sides imbued with a Cold War mentality, who have been unable to set aside their obsolete 20th-century agenda to begin a new era of co-operation.

At a cabinet level, the Peace Minister would provide a counterweight to colleagues who are responsible for the Defence Departments, and would argue that resources being devoted to the military instead be directed at conflict prevention and demilitarization. The ministry would control at least part of the national foreign aid budget, which it would use to provide post-conflict relief and to promote peaceful cultural exchanges, but also to budget for de-radicalization and community-outreach initiatives on the home front.

One of the responsibilities of the UK's Minister of Peace and Disarmament would be to brief the Prime Minister daily on the latest international peace and security situation, with alternative suggestions and advice to defuse or mediate situations where tensions are rising at home and abroad. On a monthly basis, the Peace Department would prepare a report for the Cabinet on the latest domestic and international situation on:

a) International peace and security
b) Protection of human rights
c) Progress on mitigation of the climate-change crisis
d) Poverty reduction and progress towards the Sustainable Development Goals
e) Combating terrorism through de-radicalization
f) Progress towards gender equality
g) Defence diversification strategy, action and its progress.

Rather as foreign ministers sometimes have to represent the voice of foreign powers – even unfriendly ones – the Minister for Peace would also become the voice of domestic groups whose grievances are leading towards conflict or political instability. Such a voice inside the executive would help governments to formulate inclusionary policies that avoid exacerbating societal rifts, and to avoid inadvertently inflaming these divisions with poor communications.

This advocacy at the highest level would prevent governments from underestimating the scale of public discontent, in a way that has recently aggravated the separatist crisis in Catalonia, that has seen the election of anti-system candidates in dozens of countries, and which led the British government to assume, wrongly, that it would win that country's referendum on membership of the European Union. History is littered with examples of outraged societies toppling governments led by a detached and oblivious elite class that only listens to itself. Marie Antoinette might never have advised the starving masses of France to eat cake, but this mentality persists even among the leaders of our democracies. One part of the Peace Minister's brief must be to shake leaders out of their complacency, before it inflicts real harm.

If even one such crisis could be averted as a result of the Department for Peace, it would justify its budget many times over. The costs of conflict, internal and external, run into the trillions of dollars. According to the Costs of War Project undertaken by Brown University in the US, the wars since 2001 have run up a bill of $5.6 trillion for the US taxpayer.[6] On the principle that prevention is better than cure, devoting even one per cent of tax resources to easing divisions between a society's alienated and potentially violent groups and the majority is likely to prove an investment that repays itself by many multiples.

Losses of that magnitude do not just affect poor countries; they make everyone poorer, regardless of where they live. Of course, even these financial losses pale when compared to the emotional and psychological damage inflicted by deaths and abuses as a result of conflict.

In 2017 only six countries (Britain, Sweden, Norway, Luxembourg, Denmark and the Netherlands) exceeded the UN's 0.7 per cent of its GDP target for international aid spending. Even if every country did meet that objective, it would still only be about half the total spent on military upkeep. There must be a better way.

The departments would help promote a more sophisticated concept of national security that encompasses environmental stability, enhanced economic self-sufficiency and food security as well as the security of women, children and minority groups, and to stamp out the global injustice of the grand larceny we call 'corruption'. In particular, Peace Departments must advocate against the creation or continuation of grand alliances such as NATO, the Shanghai Cooperation Organisation, and the Organisation of Islamic Cooperation, that threaten to divide the world into mutually antagonistic blocs. Rather, the Peace Departments would offer much-needed support for the United Nations and its associated system of international law.

Swords into ploughshares

Peace activists at times are guilty of issuing demands without solutions. It is beholden on us to suggest ways in which companies like Boeing and Lockheed Martin can be repurposed to peaceful ends, while preserving the state-of-the-art technology that is sometimes a positive by-product of their work. Breaking the Frame, for instance, a UK-based activist group, has launched a campaign to repurpose technology away from harmful uses and to expose the political rhetoric that disguises this harm.[7]

In September 2017, much of the Caribbean was devastated by Hurricane Irma, a Category 5 storm (which appear to be becoming ever more common). As is often the case, military units were deployed as first responders to islands that had been catastrophically damaged.

Such military units are often poorly adapted to the work of disaster relief. Britain's response to the disaster was criticized for being slow, and for some of the helicopters not being able to carry the heavy loads needed for relief operations. This was because the warships and helicopters were not purpose-built for relief operations, but for the kind of large-scale naval conflict that, thankfully, has become less common in recent decades. The ships could not approach the affected areas until the hurricane-force winds had died down.

What if companies such as BAE Systems and Raytheon focused on creating aircraft and surface vessels that could function in the extreme winds of a hurricane instead of building weapons of death? What if the personnel aboard those relief craft carried equipment for finding people trapped beneath collapsed buildings, or drones that could identify those trapped by floodwaters? What if they could deploy in the immediate aftermath of natural disasters, to act as a police force, restore law and order and prevent looting?

The US has long had a Peace Corps and this concept could be extended to encompass a disaster-response division of the US military that would contribute vastly to global perceptions of America. China, Russia and other military powers would surely follow suit, creating a virtuous competition in 'soft power' that would quickly bring their foreign aid contributions above the UN's suggested threshold, while making the world a better place.

In the longer term, such a Peace Corps could use the skills of military engineers to build roads and power stations in poor, remote areas beyond the reach of poorer national governments. The logistical and technological challenges of doing this are often enormous, but equally enormous are the scientific and technological skills of the researchers working within the military-government complex. Tasked with overcoming these obstacles, it is likely they would make progress.

Such operations would need to be conducted in co-operation within local governments. As we have seen time and again, attempts to impose a foreign definition of 'progress' on societies who feel no ownership of the process leads, at best, to the improvements degrading over time, and at worst to violent insurgency.

Space races

Another peaceful way of repurposing the military-industrial complex is exploration. Throughout the Cold War, the US and the Soviet Union competed in a 'space race' that led to humankind launching satellites and sending a cosmonaut to orbit the Earth, and culminated US astronauts walking on the moon. Cynics dismissed all this as a waste of money that should have been spent on more mundane concerns; but for many other people, such feats of courage and technology were an awe-inspiring monument to human ambition.

And space exploration often has by-products that benefit us all. Nasa's research has either initiated or contributed a breakthrough to the development of satellite navigation systems, smoke detectors, non-reflective computer displays, light-emitting diodes, ear thermometers, landmine removal and detection, fire-resistant cladding for buildings, improved crash protection for airline passengers, freeze drying, solar panels and water purification – just some of the benefits that humanity has accrued from the challenge of exploring space. Some of these scientific breakthroughs have saved untold lives.

By petitioning for the redirection of military resources into space exploration, peace activists can appeal to the patriotism and courage of military families, and the need for governments to accrue 'soft power' to support their diplomatic objectives. When Yuri Gagarin became the first human to orbit the Earth in 1961, he did so on behalf of a Soviet Union that, only five decades earlier, had been so poor and unjust that its tsar had been mocked as 'Genghis Khan with the telegraph'. Gagarin's voyage was a stunning statement of the transformative power of communism.

Other military resources can be redeployed to support the Department of Peace. Domestically, the Department for Peace would support effective community peace-building initiatives such as conflict resolution, training for police, peer mediation and conflict-resolution programmes in schools. Internationally, the Department for Peace would play a major role in prevention and de-escalation of conflicts as well as post-conflict reconstruction and reconciliation. The Department for Peace would oversee the creation and administration of Peace Centres intended to promote a culture of peace and nonviolence.

A new culture

The ultimate purpose of the Department for Peace is cultural change. It would focus taxpayer resources onto the promotion of peace and the eventual abolition of war. There should be a Culture of Peace unit in the department that pursues the programme of action outlined in the 1999 UN Declaration for a Culture of Peace. This aims to create values, attitudes and behaviours that address the root causes of violence, with a view to solving problems through dialogue and negotiations among individuals, groups and nations. The eight areas of action proposed by the declaration are:

1) **Fostering a culture of peace through education** by promoting education for all, focusing especially on girls; revising curricula to promote the qualitative values, attitudes and behaviour inherent in a culture of peace; training for conflict prevention and resolution, dialogue, consensus-building and active nonviolence.

2) **Promoting sustainable economic and social development** by targeting the eradication of poverty; focusing on the special needs of children and women; working towards environmental sustainability; fostering national and international co-operation to reduce economic and social inequalities.

3) **Promoting respect for all human rights** by distributing the Universal Declaration of Human Rights at all levels and fully implementing international instruments on human rights.

4) **Ensuring equality between women and men** by integrating a gender perspective and promoting equality in economic, social and political decision-making; eliminating all forms of discrimination and violence against women; supporting and aiding women in crisis situations resulting from war and all other forms of violence.

5) **Fostering democratic participation** by educating responsible citizens; reinforcing actions to promote democratic principles and practices; establishing and strengthening national institutions and processes that promote and sustain democracy.

6) **Advancing understanding, tolerance and solidarity** by promoting a dialogue among civilizations; actions in favour of vulnerable groups; respect for difference and cultural diversity.

7) **Supporting participatory communication and the free flow of information and knowledge** by means of such actions as support for independent media in the promotion of a culture of peace; effective use of media and mass communications; measures to address the issue of violence in the media; knowledge and information sharing through new technologies.

8) **Promoting international peace and security** through action such as the promotion of general and complete disarmament; greater involvement of women in prevention and resolution of conflicts and in promoting a culture of peace in post-conflict situations; initiatives in conflict situations; encouraging confidence-building measures and efforts for negotiating peaceful settlements.

The UN precepts build upon much older ones. The UK, for instance, should celebrate the Magna Carta, and other constitutional documents of our past cultural and social history which are foundational for understanding how we are fortunate to live in what is, by global standards, a peaceful and thus prosperous society.

Departments for Peace will act as a catalyst in stopping the military's engagement in violence and permanent wars. It will also reduce the unsustainable budget of countries for the procurement of weapons and military hardware. It will have the benefit of savings achieved from the cuts in military spending which can be redirected to creating jobs, efficient healthcare, conflict resolution and promotion of a culture of peace.

When the ambition of these goals is understood, it becomes clear why the world needs Departments of Peace. There is a very significant role for such institutions to play in the 21st century, an era that has already been wracked by internal division not just in poor and turbulent states, but in traditionally wealthy and stable ones too.

What we need to do is to create momentum with like-minded people who will become agents for change, who will make the creation of the Departments for Peace a reality.

Individual actions can make this possible if we stand up for an ideal to improve the lot of others against injustice. These actions will send tiny ripples of hope, full of energy, to create a mighty current which can tear down the walls of oppression and resistance. Each person in this world is a tiny ripple of hope and, collectively, these millions of ripples of energy will carry us all forward in building a peaceful world.

1 Lazare, Sarah, 2017, 'Federally-funded peace "institute" providing platform for war mongers and torture cheerleaders', Alternet, nin.tl/war-mongers 2 Peterson, Scott, 2016, 'Iraq's Tikrit shows the path to reconciliation', *Khaleej Times*, 23 November, nin.tl/iraqs-tikrit 3 International Centre for Transitional Justice, 2004, *Bosnia and Herzegovina: Selected Developments in Transitional Justice*, nin.tl/ictj-bosnia 4 Robinson, Michael J, 2007, 'Two Decades of American News Preferences', Pew Research Centre, nin.tl/us-news 5 Allbright, Claire, 2017, 'A Russian Facebook page organized a protest in Texas. A different Russian page launched the counterprotest', *The Texas Tribune*, 1 November, nin.tl/russia-counterprotest 6 Watson Institute, Brown University, nin.tl/us-costs 7 Breaking the Frame, 'Our Mission', breakingtheframe.org.uk/political-statement

Chapter 3

Making Peace Pay – Setting Up Social Business Enterprises in the 21st Century

Can peace pay? At first sight, this may seem a strange statement.

For decades, the peace movement has been associated with the Left of the political spectrum – activists who are naturally suspicious of the profit motive. At best, they see business figures as amoral bystanders who are unwilling or unable to advance the cause of peace. At worst, such activists view business and investors as synonymous with the military-industrial complex that drives many global conflicts. By arriving at such assumptions too easily and glibly, the cause of peace is conceding billions of dollars of potential financing to other worthy causes that, it is abundantly clear, succeed in tapping sources of private-sector revenue. Environmentalism, disease prevention, water security, anti-racism and the elimination of child labour are all movements that have successfully courted the rich and powerful.

These movements have been able to tap this enormous pool of funding because they have developed a shared lexicon with the business community. Buzzwords such as 'ecologically sustainable development', 'diversity', 'a carbon footprint', 'dignified work' and 'integrated vector management' are now every bit as well-understood in MBA programmes as they are in civil society. Corporations have realized that to modernize, they need to actively render the world a better place – particularly those corporations which, arguably, are making the world a worse place due to aspects of their business model.

The peace movement has been slow to develop the vocabulary needed to communicate effectively in the world of investors and C-suite executives. In part, this reflects the heterogeneity of our movement. There is no single explanation for what causes war. Accordingly, there is no single agreed method for preventing conflict. Contrast this situation with, say, the consensus that reducing carbon dioxide emissions is critical to reversing climate change, or that educating girls is fundamental to human development.

Nevertheless, our heterogeneity can be a strength, provided peace activists can at least agree a common lexicon with which to engage potential investors and thus mobilize their resources. When writing our glossary of terms, a good place to start is the World Bank's Environmental and Social Framework for investment, which organizations must fulfil to qualify for the Bank's loans.

It urges companies investing in fragile states to establish grievance mechanisms to avoid or mitigate adverse impacts to people; to conduct social and conflict analysis; to adhere to the Universal Declaration of Human Rights; to understand the concepts of a social audit, due diligence and duty of care; to avoid involuntary resettlement; to protect the cultural heritage of Historically Underserved Traditional Local Communities, to secure their Free, Prior and Informed Consent (FPIC) and to operate on 'do no harm' principles.

In order to communicate effectively with the corporate sector, peace activists must be prepared to talk in terms of risk ratings, and of metrics for monitoring conflict risks; the need for supporting sustainable institutions that outlast the initial funding phase; to pursue stakeholder engagement on a differentiated basis so that any adverse consequences of a company's operations do not fall disproportionately on the most vulnerable members of society; to speak in terms of capacity constraints and the way that investors and corporate leaders can help to alleviate them.

Some members of the peace movement are likely to feel

uncomfortable translating their approach into such brochure-friendly buzzwords. They might look suspiciously upon the entire process, particularly at a historical moment in which the neoliberal consensus of the 1990s and 2000s is facing complete collapse. A cynic might even suspect that corporations will simply exploit them for marketing purposes and publicity, in order to 'peacewash' the consequences of corporate rapacity.

But to think this way would be overly cynical. Indeed, it would be to make the same error as neoliberal economists. Their perpetual and damaging mistake is to think of people as emotionless, calculating 'Econs' rather than, to use the distinction made by Nobel-winning behavioural economist Richard Thaler, as humans. Because entrepreneurs, investors and fund managers are humans. Most of them have the same fears about the future of their children and their planet as everyone else. They are not always venal, self-interested and callous, any more than academics, civil servants and non-profit leaders are not always kindly, generous and considerate.

Brian J Grim, president of the Religious Freedom & Business Foundation, has outlined four ways businesses can help to build peace: Emerging Market Entrepreneurship, Social Impact-Driven Entrepreneurship, Corporate Entrepreneurship and Ecosystem for Innovation-Driven Entrepreneurship. He also observed that the peace-making potential of business is largely unreported, unstudied and untapped. More research and incentivizing programmes would help change that.

Grim emphasized the need to increase positive incentivization of 'double-bottom-lined enterprises' that do social good and make a profit. Possibilities include giving a higher profile to global programmes like the UN Global Compact and the Business for Peace Foundation, which bestows awards for such initiatives, and multiplying programmes that facilitate practical knowledge of impact investment, such as the Impact Bond Fund and Impact Investment Programme. Increasing such knowledge and incentives can inspire and give resources to a new generation of socially conscious

Peace Centres, business entrepreneurs and peace makers.

If peace activists can translate our objectives into the language of business schools, then the movement's anarchic and individualistic tendencies can be harnessed much more effectively. Every group of peace activists has their own view of the best way to prevent conflict. This gives each group a unique selling point (USP) with which to approach powerful business figures in order to persuade them to become impact-investors.

At our fingertips are the tools to reach billions, to shake the 21st century out of the complacency into which it was born and to impress on new generations that the stakes of war and peace are higher than they imagine. Perhaps one of the greatest reasons for optimism in the 21st century is a new breed of youngsters who bring an entrepreneurial flair to the world that is not directed at their own personal enrichment, but as a means of self-expression, creativity and exploration of new ideas. Unconventional 'hipster' modes of fundraising and small-scale retail have much to teach us.

Small-scale entrepreneurism is an effective means of financially supporting the peace movement while conveying the message of peace and raising awareness of contemporary conflicts. The ubiquity of digital technology means that manufacturing processes that would once have been prohibitively expensive for small-scale production can now be mobilized to manufacture everything from T-shirts, raspberry jam and jewellery to craft beers and mobile phone apps. For peace activists, the output of this craft economy can be branded to draw attention to, and raise funds for, the cause of peace.

By mobilizing in new and creative ways, and by donating our time in smart ways that make the most of our own personal expertise and creativity, we can maximize the impact and amplify our message.

Some examples help clarify this point. One success story is Building Markets, led by Jennifer Holt. A non-profit based in New York, its 'USP for peace' is that jobs are essential. As we explored in the first chapter, jobs not only provide an income for younger men who would otherwise be drawn into violence, they also provide an outlet for their time and energy, and offer them social status within their society.

Building Markets offers a matchmaking service to build supply chains between well-established companies and small and medium-sized enterprises (SMEs) in fragile or war-torn states such as Afghanistan. It vets these SMEs to find enterprises that are competitive, and then it trains their leaders how to win tender processes issued by globally active corporations and governments. Through these means, Building Markets has helped create some 69,000 paying jobs in fragile states, and has redirected some $1.6 billion towards them.

Of course, it is possible to disagree with Building Markets' view of peace-building. The most deadly conflicts in human history, the two world wars, were not obviously triggered by unemployment. Although Adolf Hitler came to power amid the economic crisis of the Great Depression, by 1937 German unemployment levels had normalized. Nor were unemployment levels high in Europe prior to the First World War, yet this did not prevent the conflict.[1]

Even those who accept the link between unemployment and conflict might reasonably question whether such job creation in Afghanistan will prevent the Taliban from recapturing Kabul, and they might note that many of the country's SMEs are located in the Dari-speaking west of the country, which has done little to contribute to the violence anyway, whereas generating jobs is far more important in the Pashtun-speaking east. They might ask whether such SMEs have a long-term chance of competing globally from a landlocked country when almost any business activity can be conducted more cheaply and safely in neighbouring China.

Nevertheless, for now such criticisms are secondary. Building Markets is an example of how peace activism can be established on a paying basis, by matching one plausible theory of conflict-reduction to investors who agree with this theory and who are in a position to provide substantial funding. Whatever an activist's approach to peace-building, the Building Markets example offers a valuable lesson in how to match that approach to wealthy, like-minded backers.

A second example is the work of interfaith groups. They worry that the roots of violence lie in social division; that the lack of social interaction between some communities allows conflict-instigators on one side to dehumanize members of the other, for instance in the Israeli-Palestinian conflict. By creating sustainable social and economic institutions that bridge the divide between communities, peace workers can effect a humanization process that reduces the appetite for violence, for instance by matching Palestinian companies in Ramallah to Israeli financiers in Tel Aviv, helping them scale their business.

So, if violent extremists provoke and take advantage of a bad economy to sow seeds of religious discord and violence, could peacemakers use good businesses to stimulate economic growth and foster interfaith understanding and peace?

A new set of case studies published by the UN Global Compact and the Religious Freedom & Business Foundation shows that the theory has some legs. Businesses in various parts of the world are addressing prejudices that feed violent extremism and terrorism. Although no single initiative is a magic bullet to end all such violence, taken together they offer a glimpse into the peacemaking potential of business. The initiatives include:

1) Using marketing to cross borders
Companies can make positive contributions to peace by mobilizing advertising campaigns that bring people of various faiths and backgrounds together, as seen in Coca-Cola's Small World campaigns. One of their marketing initiatives, for instance, linked people in Pakistan and India through Coca-Cola vending machines equipped with live video feeds.

2) Rewarding intercultural understanding

Cross-cultural dialogue and co-operation is an essential part of daily operations for transnational companies such as BMW. In collaboration with the UN Alliance of Civilizations, the BMW Group offers an annual award for organizations that create innovative approaches to intercultural understanding, including interfaith understanding and peace. Among organizations that have won this award is a tour company in the Middle East, which offers new ideas to build bridges and bring cultures together through collaborative Muslim-Jewish tourism in the Holy Lands.

3) Supporting social entrepreneurs

The business environment provides neutral ground for religious differences to give way to shared concerns of enterprise and economic development. For example, the Yola Innovation Machine in Adamawa State, Nigeria, supports companies and new entrepreneurs in conflict-affected areas to reduce extremism. Similarly, Petrobras in Brazil supports business incubation for Afro-Brazilians, creating models for how small enterprises can have a significant impact in empowering members of marginalized ethno-religious communities, including a focus on women's empowerment.

4) Boosting workforce diversity

When businesses are sensitive to the religious and cultural issues around them, they not only make reasonable accommodations for faith in the workplace, but they can also address difficult unmet social needs. Businesses in Indonesia did this by organizing a mass wedding for interfaith couples who had lived without legal status and with no ready means to become legitimately wed. By obtaining legal status, thousands of interfaith couples can now access the public health service, obtain education for their children, and have expanded opportunities for employment.[2]

Again, it is perfectly possible to take issue with a faith-based approach: it's hard to measure its success. An organization like Building Markets can quantify its wins much more easily. It is very difficult to persuade hardliners on either side to participate, or to absorb enough potential militants into the process. It may even be the case that there are real cultural differences between Israeli Jews and Palestinian Muslims, and that these differences will inflame rather than reduce mutual animosity if the groups interact more closely.

Noting the possibility of such objections simply underlines the point that the peace movement is not monolithic, and that people have different views of what works. When marketing to the private sector, this intellectual diversity is a strength, not a weakness. Peace entrepreneurs who advocate the interfaith strategy need only to identify potential sponsors and partners who are sympathetic to their approach and who are willing to co-brand and support it.

This concept of branding is important. In the modern world, an effective brand is not one that says 'we exist to make money for our shareholders'. Such an uninspiring message has little resonance with socially conscious millennials, who in the next two decades will come to control most of the world's wealth, as it cascades down to them from the baby boomer generation now nearing or in retirement.

To be credible and thus successful, today's brands must aspire to something greater than simple profit. They must align themselves with the aspirations of the people they want to buy their products. They must endeavour to reduce their carbon footprint, to use biodegradable materials in their packaging, to promote inclusivity of identity, to champion self-expression and generally align with efforts to solve humanity's shared problems, rather than exacerbating them. Participating in violence-reduction and peace-building is a rational decision for brand managers, business-development teams and procurement professionals, but to date it's an opportunity the peace movement has been slow to exploit.

One reason for this is brand risk, on both sides of the equation. A transnational enterprise that does extensive business in China will be reluctant to partner with an activist group that, as part of its work, asserts the political rights of Tibetans or highlights the many human rights violations of the Chinese government. Beijing has a record of retaliating against foreign companies it sees as endorsing critical views. In January 2018, the Marriott hotel chain had its Chinese-based website and mobile app closed by the authorities because it had listed Tibet and Taiwan as countries separate from the People's Republic in an email questionnaire.

Marriott had little choice but to apologize and bow to the government's wishes, given that China is the company's second-largest market. The abject nature of its apology, which echoed the language of the ruling Communist Party, prompted the International Campaign for Tibet to write to the company's chief executive, cautioning him against taking China's side on such sensitive questions. The incident showcased how in many cases, advocacy groups that stray into explicitly political territory cannot really partner with companies that must remain politically neutral in order to maintain their market share.

Make or break

How can this circle be squared? Peace projects that seek to co-brand with private investors must define the scope of their activities clearly, narrowly and in detail. At a contractual level, this should extend to a break clause that allows either party to withdraw from the partnership immediately if the other side acts in a way that compromises the core values of their partner.

Through such means can the reputational risk be mitigated, easing concerns on both sides that the partnership entails unacceptable breaches of either their ideological or their commercial obligations. On the peace side, it is important to have a clearly defined USP. Another approach that has been successful in raising revenue from the private and donor sectors is the 'interrupter' concept of trusted individuals in conflict-prone areas who can anticipate outbreaks of violence and then intercede with potential perpetrators before things get out of hand.

This method has yielded fruit both in rich countries such as the United States, with initiatives like Cure Violence working in deprived urban areas where gun crime is rampant, and in fragile states such as Burundi, where organizations such as Peace Direct have established networks of trusted ground-level sources who can alert decision-makers to mounting unrest. The tactical nature of such intervention ensures the donor side has little to worry about in terms of commercially damaging political fallout.

Such reputational risk is every bit as great on the non-profit side. In June 2015, the Nobel Peace Centre announced it was ending its partnership with FIFA, the governing body of world football, after FIFA's leadership became mired in a series of lurid corruption scandals. This ended the 'Handshake for Peace' initiative, whereby FIFA had donated €800,000 to the Nobel Peace Centre's budget.

In an era of social media and instant campaigning, no peace group can afford to co-brand with a commercial organization that has acted unethically. However, this consideration is not a reason to shun the for-profit sector. On the contrary, forging such partnerships focuses pressure on the for-profit side to act in accordance with its partner's values, or else risk an embarrassing breakdown in shared projects of the kind experienced by FIFA.

Companies that manage to sustain such partnerships over the long term can rightfully point to this durability as evidence of their own high ethical standards. Moreover, commercial organizations that have experienced public embarrassment due to ethical breaches are likely to be receptive to co-branding with pro-peace groups as a means of recovering their reputations under new, more enlightened leadership.

It is clear, therefore, that reputational risks can be managed in such a way as to make partnerships between the peace sector and commercial investors viable. Of course, some within the peace activist community will resist any compromise or accommodation that limits their ability to speak out on political issues, a mindset that remains essential to the movement as a whole. But it need not be the case for every initiative.

It might even be the case that there is a business opportunity that lies in ensuring these standards. One of the most successful models of diverting market mechanisms to support a good cause has been the Fair Trade movement. By harnessing the willingness of like-minded buyers to donate while they shop, Fair Trade activists defied market pressures to secure higher incomes for the growers of coffee, groundnuts and other agricultural commodities in the Global South. It offers a model for peace activists to follow.

Imagine, for a moment, a certification system for products that are ethically sourced from vulnerable or displaced communities, as a means of giving them an economic lifeline. Across the globe, there are communities whose lives have been torn apart by war. Some become refugees, such as the Rohingya fleeing Myanmar for Bangladesh, Somali refugees in Kenya or Syrian exiles in Jordan. The UN estimated that as of 2016, 65.6 million people had been forcibly displaced worldwide, a population the size of the UK.[3]

Of these, 10 million were stateless and 22.5 million were refugees (the figures included 5.3 million Palestinians categorized as 'refugees'). Of the refugees, 55 per cent were from just three countries – South Sudan, Afghanistan and Syria – and more than half were under the age of 18. And of these, fewer than 200,000 were settled during 2016.[3]

Statelessness compounds the hardship of peoples displaced by conflict, torn from the economic systems that formerly sustained them and thrust upon foreign populations who view them with as much mistrust as sympathy. Among the countries that host the majority of refugees are Ethiopia, Uganda and Lebanon – states that face their own grave economic, social and political problems.

Building economic links to those who have been marginalized by conflict is a means by which peace activists can simultaneously build awareness of the human costs of conflict and give consumers a channel by which to help support refugee populations. Somalis living in Kenya's Dadaab refugee camp, for instance, have few exportable goods they can manufacture, given the desolate area they are forced to inhabit and the restrictions placed on their movements, and even fewer means of bringing those goods to international markets.

Although building economic ties with refugees directly can be challenging, a Peace Trade labelling system could give recognition to states such as Kenya, Pakistan, the Palestinian Authority, Jordan and Uganda who host large numbers of refugees. Some of those countries, such as Kenya and Pakistan, are demanding that their Somali and Afghan refugee populations return to their war-torn homelands; if, however, their exporters were able to label their countries' goods as Peace Trade approved, and charge slightly more for them, this would give those governments a greater financial incentive to go on protecting displaced populations. There are no refugee camps, for example, in Canada or Denmark.

Such Peace Trade labelling would raise awareness among Western consumers about how little of the burden of protecting the world's refugees falls on the advanced northern hemisphere economies best able to absorb the cost. Most importantly, it allows ordinary people to contribute to the cause of peace while going about their daily business; one of the greatest challenges the peace movement faces is the constant demands on the time of younger people, and families in particular.

The Peace Trade campaign need not end there: our Departments for Peace must demand that countries that shelter large refugee populations receive preferential tariff access to Western markets. This should extend even to countries such as Iran, which hosts almost one million refugees, a relief operation that is rarely acknowledged by the Western governments who criticize Iran's theocratic regime.

Surfing a political wave

Peace activism has long been the preserve of the Left of the political spectrum. With the Left surging in the post-neoliberal democracies of the US and the UK, there is a question as to how the peace movement can assist this process of political and socio-economic change.

Now just might be an ideal moment to forge peace with the commercial sector, from a position of strength rather than weakness. By increasing interaction between the two camps, we can humanize one another, rather as interfaith groups seek to humanize mutually hostile communities. Corporate executives will learn that the Left does not, in fact, seek to impose Stalinism in the West, but rather is seeking a new model of participatory capitalism that does not marginalize vast swathes of society.

And peace activists might be surprised to discover that many corporate employees share their concerns about the devastation caused by armed conflict, and are seeking to help not as part of some cynical marketing stunt but from an honestly held belief in the importance of preventing warfare, which (outside the defence industry) means fewer commercial opportunities, trickier logistics, expensive private security contractors and higher taxes for the corporate sector.

By identifying these shared ambitions, and tapping hundreds of billions of dollars' worth of potential cash assistance, the peace movement can render itself more effective, more relevant, and more energized, while at the same time breaking down the suspicion and antagonism between the corporate sector and the political Left. As peace-building efforts go, this would be a triumph indeed.

There is no one-size-fits-all approach to peace entrepreneurship. Part of the fun is that every start-up has its own idea, its own business model that expresses the creativity and insights of the people setting up the enterprise. There are thousands of ways that social entrepreneurs can identify peace-problems and then propose peace-solutions to them. You do not need to have studied for an MBA, or wear a three-piece suit, or have a skin as thick as a rhino's to ask those with wealth to assist in solving these problems. Just ask them. Keep asking until one says yes.

Peace Centres will broadly focus on six main areas that go together to build peace:

- Disarmament and Demilitarization
- Conflict Prevention and Resolution
- Economic and Social Justice
- Human Rights, Rule of Law and Democracy
- Environment and Sustainable Development
- Promotion and Implementation of a Culture of Peace and Nonviolence

Without being prescriptive, this chapter outlines a few broad areas of activity in which social enterprise can lessen the risks of violent conflict. Readers will undoubtedly think of more, but as a way of getting the intellectual ball rolling, the following ideas may be of assistance.

Connecting the strong to the fragile

As noted, there isn't much of a consensus on the fundamental causes of war, any more than there is a consensus on the fundamental causes of fist-fights. In a world of standing armies, cruise missiles and nuclear submarines primed to a state of constant readiness, war is baked into the cake of our existence. Starting wars requires no more preparation or forethought than it does for one drunk person to punch another.

The best we can say, in regards to consensus, is that in the modern world conflict is usually a result of groups being economically, socially or politically excluded from the mainstream of national or international society. This

definition is unhelpfully broad, but it shines a spotlight on
a problem that peace enterprises can potentially solve: how
to include people in such a way that the urge to react with
violence dissipates.

Working together

Peace activists can connect conflict-prone groups to the global
economy. Often, this will also entail upskilling members of
those communities so they have the wherewithal to trade
on an equal footing with the wider world. Crucially, peace
activists can provide insights into Western cultures that will
make it easier for such communities to market their talents.
By strengthening the economic power of minorities who are at
persistent risk of armed conflict with the state, peace activists
can help defuse the scope for unrest.

It is worth noting that, contrary to popular belief, even
major companies are willing to engage with fragile states.
Consider for a moment that, according to the British
government, the Palestinian Territories already host major UK
businesses such as PwC, HSBC and BG Group, alongside a host
of smaller British companies.[4] Their participation in Palestine
has been incentivized by the European Union, which has
granted the Palestinian Territories preferential trade terms.

The British government perceives further investment
opportunities for high-value agriculture, business process
outsourcing, tourism and goods trade in the Palestinian
Territories, all of which would lessen the Ramallah
government's reliance on foreign financial support, while
reducing both the economic power of militant groups funded
by Iran, and Israel's economic stranglehold over Palestine.
The British guidance notes that the Palestinian Territories
have some clear advantages for global trade, with an educated
population, connective geography and widely spoken English.

Next door is Lebanon, a complex and conflict-prone state.
The presence of the militant group Hizbullah within the
government complicates the country's investment profile,

particularly for very large investors, but this provides an opportunity for smaller and more knowledgeable impact investors seeking to ensure that their activities in Lebanon do nothing to aggravate the country's complex sectarian equations, but rather support prosperity in a way that consolidates peace and social cohesion in the formerly war-torn state.

Activists looking to build these kind of economic bridges need not work in the dark. UNCTAD, the UN's trade and investment arm, has produced a list of best practices for investing in post-conflict states.[5] It argues that even though foreign investment alone cannot bring peace or prosperity, such investment helps to *solidify* the peace. This is crucial: as former UN chief Kofi Annan observed, half of states that sign a peace accord lapse back into violence within five years.

One challenge identified by the UN is often the shortage of skilled labour in post-conflict states. Peace activists can potentially play a role by liaising between potential investors and networks of skilled refugees who have fled to Europe and North America but who are interested in helping rebuild their homelands. This can lessen the risk-adversity of transnational enterprises towards post-conflict environments.

Often, skilled members of a refugee diaspora are forced by circumstance to work in professions that do not reflect their qualifications, with engineers driving taxis and doctors working as hospital porters. This can lead to an erosion of personal skills. A useful role for peace entrepreneurs, then, might be connecting such skilled refugees to mentors and educational courses that allow them to refresh their knowledge.

Activists can play matchmaker between companies that have survived their domestic conflict and potential overseas partners. This involves compiling a registry of these surviving businesses, their activity and reliable means by which to contact their leaders. It is also helpful to understand whether these business leaders have personal relationships with current or former political leaders, as such 'politically exposed persons' can open foreign investors to charges of corruption if the relationships are not fully disclosed and subject to due diligence.

Quality food exports can provide an economic lifeline for post-conflict countries. Among the main exports of Sierra Leone, a West African country that endured civil war between 1991 and 2002, is honey. By helping Sierra Leone's beekeepers market their honey to buyers in developed markets, peace activists can alleviate poverty in the country while supporting its ecosystem, to which bees are crucial. Socially aware Western customers are likely to be willing to pay more for a product they know is helping to consolidate peace and sustainability in West Africa. This is a blend of commerce, environmentalism and charity that makes for a compelling business proposition.

Activists with extensive local knowledge are well placed to identify which parts of a country survived the conflict relatively intact and could thus serve as a beachhead for transnational corporations to establish a base of operations. However, UNCTAD notes that such corporations often prefer a 'low contact' approach before committing major funds to an investment.[5]

With that in mind, it is worth noting that many countries offer entrepreneur visas, which allow foreign nationals to establish a business providing certain financial requirements are met. Colombia, a country recovering from decades of conflict, grants a TP-7 visa to entrepreneurs willing to invest the equivalent of 100 times the minimum monthly salary, a sum equivalent to around $26,000 at the time of writing. Although the application process is time-consuming and unpredictable, it gives foreign nationals with a clear business plan the opportunity to invest directly in Colombia and travel there as a resident.

As part of their mission, Peace Centres promote a culture of peace, a multicultural environment in which conflicts can be resolved in a respectful, peaceful way in accordance to 'house rules'. Workshops on conflict resolution provide an educational element to the work of Peace Centres, often expressed through theatre, music or art, with trained and vetted adult volunteers and mentors working with young people to socialize them into mainstream society.

It should be noted that governments are already spending vast sums on the issues that Peace Centres address. The UK's 2018 budget announced school projects in Northern Ireland worth £300m, which would increase the provision of shared and integrated cross-community education. The money is already there and already being used, but it needs to be a permanent fixture of annual budgets – not a discretionary one.

One parallel is with the UK's controversial 'free schools' experiment, which allows groups of engaged parents, teachers or charities to establish their own schools and seek public funding for them. While operating a similarly de-centralized model, the Peace Centres would only be established in areas of need, and they would source funding from large corporations and local businesses rather than the general taxpayer. One can also tap into huge pension and sovereign funds and impact finance which can be utilized to solve some of the most pressing global problems – like ending conflicts, poverty reduction and global warming.

By promoting social inclusion, Peace Centres can tackle some of the root causes of conflict worldwide. By liaising with the government and private-sector marketing directors to create the budget, vision and leadership for Peace Centres, peace entrepreneurs can do *real* good.

It is possible to bring about change rapidly as billions of us are now interconnected via the internet and social media. Peace Centres can trigger change by initiating grassroots movements and actions not witnessed by anyone before. Such collective transformation for an equitable and peaceful world through the establishment of Departments for Peace and Peace Centres is the best hope we have for change to happen. So let us all be agents of change to bring it around.

1 NBER, 'International Comparison of Unemployment Rates', nber. org/chapters/c2649.pdf **2** The World Bank, 'Environmental and Social Frameworks', nin.tl/worldbank-esf **3** UNHCR, Global Trends 2016, unhcr. org/globaltrends2016 **4** Gov.uk, 2015, 'Doing business in the Palestinian Territories: Palestinian Territories trade and export guide', Department for International Trade, 11 May, nin.tl/palestinian-territories **5** United Nations Conference on Trade and Development, 'Best Practices in Investment for Development', nin.tl/invest-for-dev

Chapter 4

Peace Centres and What They Do

Serious violence is generally perpetrated by young males, whether as child soldiers, teenage gang members or soldiers in their twenties. It is not misandrist to point this out – it is a fact. The ongoing crisis of masculinity is one that peace activists must be prepared to address if we are to achieve a less violent world.

In English schools, boys are three times more likely to be excluded than girls the same age.[1] They are most likely to be excluded between 13 and 14 years old, when antisocial behaviour peaks. The most common reasons for exclusion are persistent disruptive behaviour (29 per cent) and physical assault against other children and adults (27 per cent).

Later on in life, incarceration statistics tell an even starker tale. According to the World Prison Brief, 93 per cent of prison inmates are male. When it comes to violence inflicted against the self, males are the greatest victims. In the UK, men are three times more likely to take their own life than women, and suicide is the main cause of death for men below the age of 50.

Men and boys are in crisis. The fact that men occupy most of the world's positions of power and wealth does not alter or mitigate this fact. On the contrary, if anything, it simply forces poorer, socially marginalized males to confront their own relative 'failure'. Were women more visible at the commanding heights of society, men would feel less as if they were being judged negatively against the inherited archetypes of family patriarchy or, failing that, the fraternal warrior concept.

It is often observed that teenagers have a tendency to

become alienated from mainstream society and from their immediate family. Scientists have observed such behaviour among chimpanzees and orangutans. In this vacuum, adolescents create new 'families' drawn from friends their own age, bonding over shared interests and pastimes.

Affluent families have the resources to mitigate the risks surrounding such behaviour. Civil society and well-funded schools can organize a wide variety of sport- and skills-based clubs in which teenagers can participate. Those teenagers who view even those structures as too regimented can congregate online through social media and video games, from the safety of their bedrooms.

The risks facing poorer adolescents are even more severe. Lacking support offered by wealthier parents, they socialize in public parks, on street corners and in wasteland and derelict buildings. Boredom is a problem. Given teenagers' psychological tendency towards risk-taking, the leap into anti-social behaviour and criminality is a very short one.

This is particularly true because groups of bored and impoverished teenage boys are attractive recruits for organized criminals. Gangs that transport illegal drugs across international borders require sales assistants if they are to make a profit. They lure teenage boys with a 'family' structure that promises prestige, excitement and the (remote) possibility of wealth. It is a compelling, mendacious proposition.

This is why the 'social inclusion' element of impact-investing is so critically important. The role of capitalism is to deliver to the masses what was once available only to the rich. In the 1700s, only the wealthiest had horses and carriages, but today many people have bicycles, cars and access to public transport. Where pineapple was once an exotic luxury in Europe, now the fruit is affordable for almost any budget. Where once only the rich could afford foreign travel, the expansion of cheap airlines has opened it to the masses.

To foster social inclusion, peace activists must find ways of giving poor adolescents the same opportunities for law-abiding entertainment and socializing that are available to wealthier ones. The creation of Peace Centres is therefore of paramount importance.

In Costa Rica, the vice-ministry of peace has established civic Peace Centres in each of the country's seven provinces. These focus on children and adolescents, equipping them with skills that strengthen Costa Rica's social fabric and further reduce the scope for criminal or civil violence. The Centres incorporate dance workshops, auditoriums, sports areas, skate parks and meeting rooms. Crucially, they provide a safe environment for youths to congregate and socialize while avoiding the horrendous rates of street violence and murder that plague other Central American countries such as Honduras, El Salvador and Guatemala.

Peace Centres provide a safe space for adolescents to congregate. They exclude criminals who wish to recruit youths into selling drugs, intimidating rival gangs, prostitution, car theft or shoplifting. Socially, the Centres provide the same range of entertaining diversions and structured activities that are offered to wealthier teenagers – everything from paddleboarding and skateboard parks to virtual-reality gaming suites. By offering an environment that is more fun than anything available on the streets, the Peace Centres prevent young males in particular from embarking on a devastating series of life choices that exclude them from society not only as teenagers, but for life.

Firm foundations

Establishing such Centres is well within the capability of a leftwing government, such as one led by the Labour Party in the UK or the Democratic Party in the US. A much bigger question is what happens when a leftwing government loses an election and is replaced by a rightwing one. It is likely that parties such as the US Republicans, Canada's Conservatives or Australia's rightwing Liberal Party would simply abolish the Peace Centres as soon as they got the chance. How do we prevent this?

Here we can learn from 'free schools'. This experiment, which originated in Sweden, allows groups of engaged parents, teachers and/or charities to establish their own schools and seek public funding for them, rather than schools being established according to a central planning process. The idea is controversial, with Britain's Labour Party describing them as a 'dangerous ideological experiment'. But much as the Labour Party dislikes the policy, it becomes very difficult to abolish such experiments once they are already full of teenagers receiving an education. The difficulty of re-distributing the pupils to other schools becomes just too great. Because of this, Labour has promised only to block the creation of any new free schools, rather than closing the ones already in existence.

To institutionalize Peace Centres in the same way requires a radical approach. If they are no different from youth centres, many of which already exist, they can be starved of funding by a hostile government, or simply shut down. To prevent this the Peace Centres must be woven into the threads of everyday life, in such a way that no incoming government can simply scrap or de-fund them without encountering huge public opposition.

Achieving this is possible, but it requires a degree of radicalism. Thankfully, such new thinking is finally at hand. John McDonnell, Labour's Shadow Chancellor, has mooted moving the British workforce to a four-day week. This offers one way that, perhaps, the Peace Centres can be rendered indispensable. What if schools only taught lessons for four days a week, with the fifth spent in the new Peace Centres?

Rolling out this new system would make most immediate sense somewhere like Northern Ireland, where the segregation of schools along Catholic and Protestant lines continues to breed suspicion between the communities that risks reviving the violence of the Troubles. Only seven per cent of schools in the North are desegregated.[2] Requiring schools, for one day a week, to share the same space, participate in shared clubs and sports, and receive a peace-based education that generates a shared understanding of historical narratives and grievances would go a long way to breaking the sectarian separation of schools, while at the same time respecting parents' wishes for a religious education for their children.

Northern Ireland is just an extreme instance of a problem found across Europe and the wider world. In many European towns and cities, schools have *de facto* segregation along ethnic and religious lines – a problem that ranges from Yorkshire and Paris to Frankfurt and Malmö. Often, the composition of a school's intake reflects the 'ghettoization' of a particular minority in the surrounding area, or the so-called 'white flight' from an area that was previously mixed.

Imagine if for one day a week, say a Wednesday, pupils from across a city or county congregated at their local Peace Centre. Rather than the very narrow selection of sports and clubs that individual schools are able to provide, the Peace Centre would offer everything from board-game clubs and debating societies to cinema screenings and book groups, BMX biking circuits and cricket teams. The sheer diversity of activities is crucial in order to create small, activity-based clubs that bring together members from across divided communities. Chess has no race or religion, nor does trampolining, or needlework, or sculpture, or karate.

How does this foster peace? It does so by cutting across sectarian and ethnic lines. By forging friendships outside the ruts laid down by the socio-economic system. By humanizing groups that otherwise lie outside of each other's society. By introducing French Catholics to French Arabs. By placing Germans and Turkish-Germans in the same classrooms and clubs. By uniting people around their shared interests, rather than dividing them by their backgrounds.

The Peace Centres would also address these divisions in more direct ways. Included in the Wednesday timetable would be peace symposiums that draw together individuals from across social divides, to debate and analyse why their communities live apart. These classes would encompass civic education, ensuring that all young people, regardless of their family background, are fully aware of their rights as members of that society. Women's rights, and the need to respect the rights of the disabled, ethnic minorities and the LGBTQ community, would be central to the education, in order to create a strong, mainstream culture of respect. It would allow for multiculturalism, rather than the parallel monocultures that divide many cities.

Many police forces in the US and Europe require officers to undertake cultural sensitivity training; rolling this out for everyone is a path to a more peaceful world. The effectiveness of such education is maximized in classes that attract a diversity of attendees, rather than in schools that have been *de facto* segregated by ethnicity, religion or – most often – by income. By placing individuals from mutually isolated communities in the same room, they humanize each other, fostering the empathy needed to reject narratives of hostility that divided cities into 'us' and 'them'.

Peace Centres can trigger change by initiating grassroots movements and actions not witnessed by anyone before. With strong telecommunications links, the Centres can connect young people via video to their peers in almost any country in the world. This offers a means of breaking down harmful preconceptions not just at a local level, but globally too.

Healing social gulfs would be every bit as central to this process as ethnic or religious ones, with weekly attendance at the Peace Centres mandatory not only for state-funded schools, but for private ones too. Britain in particular suffers from a 'ghettoization' by class, with a ruling elite, mostly educated in residential boarding schools, who sometimes seem oblivious to the needs of less well-off people and befuddled by their political choices. Eroding segregation by income, and addressing animosity between social classes, would be one of the main ways that Peace Centres could build societal trust – by breaking down social barriers.

Such geographical consolidation of extra-curricular school

activities also makes sense in terms of social and gender equality. Fewer and fewer schools, particularly in urban areas, have the playing fields and other facilities necessary to accommodate a wide range of athletics. Nor, given the demands placed on teachers' time, can they offer more than a narrow range of sports and clubs. This in itself is a source of social conflict. The parents of girls, for instance, might reasonably question why they have to organize and pay for their daughters' ballet classes out of school hours, while football, an activity more popular among boys, is offered by schools for free. Large, municipal-scale Peace Centres would end this unfairness by providing equal access to both.

Bringing an end to the culture wars

The rationing of places in school sporting teams is also a source of social discord as not everyone can be on the football team. In a state-funded setting, this can look unfair, with more public resources being expended on some individuals than on others – a problem that is compounded by the unfair advantage that many sports confer on taller individuals, and those born earlier in the school year and who are thus older and perhaps stronger than their peers. American sports such as gridiron football and basketball all confer an advantage on players who are of above-average height.

Americans call athletically gifted people 'jocks', and those more inclined to academics 'nerds'. Popular culture presents these two groups as inimical to one another. Although absurdly reductive – most Americans cannot neatly be described as either a jock or a nerd – this binary animosity, endlessly portrayed by US popular culture, inflames the so-called culture wars between Republicans and Democrats, between Christians and secularists, males and females. It shouldn't be important, but it is.

Republicans are, as a political party, the jocks. They view the US military as an extension of the football field, a uniform-clad strategic and tactical theatre which they see, like Aristotle, as a place where masculine virtues can be showcased. Their worldview venerates physical and psychological strength and success, and despises weakness and unorthodoxy. Men play the sport; women are cheerleaders on the sidelines, dancing and waving pom-poms.

The Democrats are the party of nerds. They define themselves in opposition to this macho Republican worldview, and they champion the interests of those who fall outside its vision of a stratified, male-dominated society that imposes conformity through a single version of 'success'. They align with the underdog, even when the underdog's behaviour is not necessarily admirable or unproblematic, or if it is even correct or respectful to consider them as underdogs.

In 2018, this culture war played out in the confirmation hearings of the US's Supreme Court justice, Brett Kavanaugh. Late on in his hearings, Democrats laid out allegations that, as a teenager in the early 1980s, Kavanaugh had bundled a teenage girl into a bedroom and attempted to undress her without her consent, although she quickly escaped. The allegations fed into a wider societal debate, popularized by the #MeToo movement, about the treatment of women, not least by the man who had nominated Kavanaugh, President Donald J Trump.

But the Democrats were also doing something else. They were highlighting that Kavanaugh was a jock. His high school yearbook entry was picked over by senators and the media and was a long list of Kavanaugh's sporting triumphs, keg and beach parties, namechecks of his jock friends, and obscure (possibly sexual) slang. In words that are now permanently inscribed in congressional testimony, an embarrassed Kavanaugh explained to the confirmation committee that:

'I think some editors and students wanted the yearbook to be some combination of Animal House, Caddyshack and Fast Times at Ridgemont High, which were all recent movies at that time. Many of us went along in the yearbook to the point

of absurdity. This past week, my friends and I have cringed when we read about it and talked to each other.[3]

Kavanaugh's testimony illustrated the nexus between Hollywood depictions of the jock-nerd dynamic, the potential for abusive behaviour resulting from the prevailing culture informed by popular culture, and the very long-lasting political and emotional damage it can inflict, throughout a human lifetime. Kavanaugh and his accuser Christine Blasey Ford, a psychology lecturer at Palo Alto University, were both in their fifties when the allegations came to light.

How can Peace Centres break this dynamic? Simply, by removing sporting teams from the educational domain, and placing them in a club setting in which they are played for the love of the game itself, not in order to secure social superiority over classmates, or to create a ready-made circle of bullies who can abuse 'weaker' individuals. It should of course be noted that by no means all school sporting stars are abusive bullies. Nevertheless, Peace Centres would provide an opportunity to once and for all break the connection between organized sport and toxic masculinity.

The Peace Centres would permit schools to specialize in academic education, without any expectation that hard-pressed teachers should devote their time, out of hours, to refereeing not only sports but the complex jostling for social hierarchy that comes with team selection. By ending the rationing of places in sporting teams – the Peace Centres would be large enough to accommodate dozens of club teams, for all manner of sports – schools could then foster an egalitarian atmosphere that does not encourage athletes to think of themselves as superior to their peers, or entitled to preferential treatment by teachers or classmates.

And although most of the problems associated with violence and war are related to male psychology, Peace Centres can also disrupt the patterns of female bullying, too, which tends to operate more often around social exclusion than physical threats. Most adults have friends from outside their workplace. This is not necessarily the case with teenagers. School is often their entire social and professional world, in a way that can often become psychologically oppressive – especially given that they cannot simply 'resign' if they find their peers unpleasant.

By creating friendship groups that run parallel to those in the classroom, Peace Centres can alleviate the at times suffocating social pressure that comes with schools operating as the sole social and academic milieu for adolescents. This could help to alleviate the wave of psychological illness and self-harm that is afflicting teenagers, particularly girls, across many Western countries. Ultimately, it reduces the unhappiness in adulthood that often manifests itself in support for harmful political ideologies.

There are other ways in which Peace Centres can help end the culture wars. Academic education is often difficult to combine with fostering the 'soft skills' needed to thrive in a human environment: the appreciation of other people's points of view, the care with which humour needs to be deployed to avoid causing offence, how easy it is to accidentally offend someone by carelessly assuming that everyone in a room lives a life much like one's own.

The Centres' curriculums can thus be designed to foster non-academic skills in teenagers, to complement the academic education they receive in school. The idea is to replicate for the masses the kind of all-round range of clubs, societies and pastimes that are currently available only to the pupils of the most expensive boarding schools; schools whose alumni often go on to dominate the most desirable, well-paid professions.

The budgetary case

At this point, we run into political reality: Peace Centres could be deemed expensive. They are no such thing when compared to the staggering costs of the military, but they are costly in the context of Western political debate. Some of the expenses of establishing Peace Centres can be met by redirecting huge amounts of money now spent on arms and the military. A tragic paradox is that the inner-city areas where gang violence is most common have land values much higher than those of more peaceful rural areas. Simply re-developing existing public parks is unfeasible. Headlines such as 'Taxpayers pick up bill for gang members' virtual reality' or 'Local park concreted for skateboarders' are inevitable among sections of the press.

Changing the political mindset around 'affordability' is a longstanding objective of peace campaigners. How can it be 'affordable' for the US to operate 10 aircraft carrier fleets simultaneously, but 'unaffordable' to do anything to pre-empt the 650 murders that Chicago saw in 2017? That's more than 20 times the number of US combat personnel who lost their lives that year. If vast expenditure can keep US soldiers safe in war zones, why can't it protect the young people of Chicago? As we noted earlier, it is time we changed the way we measure prosperity.

Additionally, the Peace Centres cannot simply close at weekends or during school holidays if they are to be effective. Those are the times the Centres are most needed. Public transport services must be made available to young people and their parents so the Centres are accessible even to those on low incomes. And the Peace Centres need to be physically large enough to accommodate several thousand young people at a time – much larger than an average school campus in Europe. Very few schools can boast a swimming pool, music studio, sports fields, virtual-reality suite, skateboard park, dance gym, theatre, cinema, kayaking facilities, tennis courts and bowling lanes. This is the level of ambition required.

But despite these requirements, Peace Centres could *save* the public money. It is inefficient for every school to maintain its own separate facilities for indoor and outdoor sports, crafts and activities on its own site, particularly in urban areas with high land values. Selling inner-city sports fields for housing development is often portrayed as a tragedy. The real tragedy is the lack of vision and investment in large, purpose-built facilities such as Peace Centres which can be used by multiple schools and can cater for a much wider range of interests and aptitudes.

Unlike schools, Peace Centres should also be able to seek corporate sponsorship. Many international clothing, technology and drinks brands seek to align themselves with young people from urban communities and/or disadvantaged backgrounds. Soft drinks manufacturers in particular are accused of increasing obesity rates, so being able to sponsor youth projects that not only promote peace but also encourage physical fitness is a compelling marketing proposition for such companies, worldwide.

In 2013, former UN Secretary General Ban Ki-moon set up the Businesses for Peace Platform to harness the largely untapped potential of businesses to bring peace while companies grow their bottom lines. He further said that because businesses are at the crossroads of culture, commerce and creativity, they have the resources and incentive to make the world more peaceful. This kind of initiative is precisely the means to link the corporate sector to the funding of Peace Centres.

The Department for Peace must play a key role in identifying the areas of highest need, presenting the short- and long-term costings (in line with the potential impact on the community/individuals), expediting the planning process, setting minimum standards, certifying staff, assessing their effect on crime rates and inspecting the facilities to ensure they are compliant. However, it can also help to drum up private sponsorship. Investing in the Peace Centres could be made tax-deductible for those businesses supporting the Centres.

The long-term financial gains would be even more profound. By keeping vulnerable young people off the streets, the Peace Centres would frustrate and forestall many forms of criminal activity. The savings on policing and incarceration would run into the billions. And then there are the incalculable, yet unquestionably significant, financial gains from ensuring that young lives are not forever blighted by poor decisions made in adolescence.

Managed properly, and redeploying existing school-level resources more efficiently, there is no reason why the Peace Centres should not be budget-neutral or even net positive for the taxpayer, given the efficiency gains from centralizing activities that many schools and other organizations are attempting to orchestrate at a micro-level. At the very least, a Department for Peace should task civil servants with conducting a cost-benefit analysis to understand what savings can be made. Thereafter, the first Centres should be piloted in the areas of most need, where their benefits can be most immediately seen.

The only way we can secure a better future is by investing in young people. Antiquated ideas that they should learn at the 'university of life' or 'school of hard knocks' will only reproduce the same violent problems that our societies have bred for millennia. No politician will ever be condemned for making the investment to break this cycle, or for ensuring that poorer young people have the same opportunities as richer ones. Peace Centres have the power to transform our countries for the better.

---

1 Gov.uk, 2009/10, *A Profile of Pupil Exclusions in England*, Department of Education, nin.tl/pupil-exclusion 2 Rutherford, Adrian and Fergus, Lindsay, 2013, 'Public mood in Northern Ireland is for an end to segregation in schools', *Belfast Telegraph*, 26 June, nin.tl/ireland-segregation 3 Transcript, Senate Judiciary Committee, US Senate, 25 September 2018, nin.tl/BMK-interview

Chapter 5

GDP for Peace

The concept of economic 'growth' is among the most dangerous facing humanity. One task for our putative Departments for Peace should be to seek the reform of national accounts so that they include only constructive economic activity, not destructive endeavours. Stated boldly, our notion of the economy, which is generally synonymous with aggregate gross domestic product (GDP), should not count the activities of arms manufacturers.

Does this seem like an unwarranted intervention in econometrics? It shouldn't. The economist who devised GDP, Simon Kuznets, was adamant that defence spending should not be part of the calculation. As the *Financial Times'* David Pilling notes in his 2018 book *The Growth Delusion*, Kuznets, a Jewish émigré whose family had fled the Russian civil war, believed that, in peacetime, a country's ability to wage war did not contribute to people's welfare. National income statements, he wrote in 1937, should be constructed from the viewpoint of an 'enlightened social philosophy' that discounts activities that are detrimental or, in his words, a 'disservice' to society. The first item he listed for exclusion was 'all expenses on armament'.

Kuznets was clear on why this was the case. Spending on preparations for war 'subtracted from a nation's wellbeing because it reduced individuals' capacity to consume and because it was defensive in nature'. Kuznets, in fact, believed that such spending should be *subtracted* from national accounts, rather than counted as a positive output. Alas, his viewpoint was overwhelmed by the accounting practices embedded by the world wars.

Re-drafting our concept of prosperity is a vital project that extends far beyond the remit of our Departments for Peace alone. Nevertheless, the Departments should play a role in re-forging GDP to reflect only constructive activity, as Kuznets originally intended. As well as military expenditure, the costs of rebuilding after a terrorist attack, or a natural disaster, or clearing up oil spills, should not be counted as 'economic output' either. Nor should the energy expended on the air conditioners needed to keep cool in hot countries, or the radiators needed to keep warm in cold ones. All these are a deadweight loss on the public welfare.

A granular analysis demonstrates the extent to which the 'economic gains' of the arms industry are an illusion. Matt Kennard and Mark Curtis in their article 'Britain's warfare state' asked a pertinent question: is the military-industrial complex truly an economic positive?[1] Could the 26,000 highly skilled researchers, designers and engineers currently working in the military sector be more profitably employed elsewhere?

They cited a 2011 study by the University of Massachusetts, which found that every $1 billion spent on clean energy, healthcare and education created 140 per cent more jobs than $1 billion spent on the military. Other reports, they admitted, showed the opposite, at least in a British context, though they noted that in any case, employment in the arms industry is already falling as a result of high technology components, automated production and global supply lines.[2]

Trade unions are understandably cautious about policies that might reduce stable, reasonably paid employment, but in this case the umbrella union Unite – Britain's second-largest trade union – supports the idea of what it calls 'a legally binding programme of diversification to kick in, retaining critical skills and finding new work for existing workers'.[2] It says this will require government intervention, and that this could fall foul of state aid and competition laws. In this particular instance, it is possible that the UK's departure from the European Union might expand the scope for action.

As we have seen, outside of the EU, Britain won't be able to rely on free trade – with Trump making that all too clear. One sensible precaution would be to enhance the country's security in a more enlightened, non-military fashion by reducing its reliance on imported energy and technology. Unite's report also highlighted how offshore renewable energy is an avenue which could achieve this while diverting employment into high-tech, high-value work.

Such policies require thinking about 'security' in a way that goes far beyond guns and tanks, but which encompasses manufacturing capacity and agricultural needs – forms of security that British policymakers have for decades neglected in their obsessive pursuit of higher GDP growth. The denial of Kuznets' vision for GDP, as a calculation that only counts beneficial spending, is only one of many ways in which the use of macro-economics has been perverted against the public interest. Adam Smith, the Glaswegian philosopher often seen as the founder of economics, placed a great deal of faith in the wisdom of ordinary people. He was highly sceptical of attempts by intellectuals to impose top-down systems that violated ordinary notions of common sense.[3] Yet today, governments, thinktanks and pundits of every kind insist that GDP growth is the only valid litmus test of good governance; exactly the kind of ideology of which Smith was most suspicious.

Humankind has fallen into the dystopian trap foreseen by Aldous Huxley in his 1931 novel *A Brave New World*. We have succumbed to Huxley's invented ideology of 'Fordism', which insists on ever-greater production and consumption. As one of the novel's characters says, observing a group of children:

> *'Imagine the folly of allowing people to play elaborate games which do nothing whatever to increase consumption. It's madness. Nowadays the Controllers won't approve of any new game unless it can be shown it requires at least as much apparatus as the most complicated existing games.'*[4]

Huxley's satire was a response to Keynes, who emphasized the importance of consumption. Today, economic Fordism has become entrenched in the Western media narrative. Growth is always good. Recession (negative growth) is reported like it's a natural disaster. Few journalists have either the training or the time to understand that for ordinary people, growth does not necessarily deliver improvements in income. Between 2007 and 2015, the British economy grew while average wages fell.[5]

It is becoming increasingly obvious that the proceeds of this 'growth' are pocketed not by workers, but by their employers. They have reaped the huge profits available in globalized markets. At the same time, they have cut their staff costs with robotics, computer programs and low-cost labour. The 'growth' narrative is little more than an insistence that the rich should get even richer. In the West at least, it has little relevance for the poor.

Even more shocking is what happens when we apply Kuznets' arms-subtraction version of GDP to modern economies. In other words, what happens when we *deduct* military spending from the GDP number, rather than adding it as if it were somehow beneficial? The results upend our understanding of the global economy. Suddenly, some countries that are currently perceived as 'rich' look much less so.

Global arms sales were almost $400 billion in 2016, with US manufacturers accounting for more than half of that total. The US government's budget for military expenditure is running at $700 billion a year,[6] with a further $60 billion for non-military intelligence spending.[7] The US spends a further $180 billion a year on policing and incarceration.[8] Additional expenditure on military and security-related budgets such as the Department of Veterans' Affairs adds another $180 billion.[9]

Added together, the costs to the US taxpayer run to over $1.1 trillion a year. At the moment, due to the way GDP is calculated, this is simply added to the total, within the 'government expenditure' component. The other three components of GDP are as follows:

- private expenditure for consumption – in other words, what ordinary people choose to buy;

- money that is invested;
- exports minus imports.

If a country's imports are greater than its exports, the difference is subtracted from the GDP. This is worth noting because it shows that subtracting from the GDP arithmetic is already part of the process.

So what happens to US GDP if security expenditure is treated as a minus rather than a plus? Rather than total US GDP equalling $19 trillion, as per the World Bank figures in 2017,[10] it falls to $17 trillion. Suddenly, Americans are 10 per cent poorer than the current statistics portray them to be.

This helps to explain the slight sense of mystification felt by many people from Europe, Japan and elsewhere when they arrive in the US to find that, to their surprise, it does not *seem* particularly wealthy, an impression that strengthens the further one strays from the very largest American cities. It helps to explain why vagrants are so visible on the streets, why derelict buildings go undemolished, why major highways are badly potholed. It helps to explain why, when it comes to everything from obesity rates[11] to urban violence to inequality rates to deaths from drinking contaminated water,[12] the numbers for the US often align more with developing countries than with rich ones. No society on earth can afford to waste a trillion dollars every year.

Counting security expenses as an economic negative, rather than a positive, would help to re-align GDP with real life. No-one can seriously believe that because a billionaire hires a close protection team to guard their family, or fits expensive security gates and cameras to their home, or drives a bullet-proof car, these expenditures make them *richer*. By the same token, societies that are forced to dedicate huge sums to security must logically be poorer than those with similar levels of income but which face no external threats, so they can spend their money on things they actually desire.

GDP misleads us into thinking that some countries are

richer than they really are, and that others are poorer than they really are. This miscalculation is itself a source of mutual suspicion, animosity and conflict. Are we really saying that a family in upstate Michigan, being slowly poisoned by water contaminated by lead, and which now subsists on benefits after its breadwinner lost a leg in Afghanistan, is really 'better off' than an average family in Argentina or Malaysia?

The Western elite's naïve belief that GDP gives a truthful picture of material wellbeing is one of the main reasons for the rise in populism. British voters elected to leave the EU after the Remain campaign employed a strategy that can be summarized as: 'Britain is wonderfully prosperous, don't jeopardize that by voting for Brexit.' In shattered post-industrial towns across non-London England and Wales, this message provoked anger and mystification, rather than support.

A closer look at the regional figures may have helped the Remain camp avoid this blunder. According to the EU's own assessment of per capita GDP, 12 of the 20 poorest regions in the northern part of the EU are in the UK.[13] How did that happen? In terms of climate and geography, Britain and Northern Ireland are similarly situated to countries such as Denmark, France, Sweden, Belgium and Germany. How have the British ended up so much poorer?

Britain's political parties and partisans simply blame each other. Usually, one side will lay the blame squarely at the 'loony Left' governments of the 1970s; the other will blame the brutal deindustrialization overseen by the rightwing Thatcher era of the 1980s. Neither side ever seems to make the connection to the cost to the public purse of Britain's bloated military and intelligence fraternity. There is no party-political advantage in making this case, because both sides have adopted a similar militaristic approach over the decades.

As a consequence of this bipartisan failing, the British spend almost twice as much of their wealth on defence as Germany.[14] As of June 2017, the UK was one of only six nations to meet

NATO spending standards for military outlay; the others were the US, Estonia, Poland, Romania and Greece (another country whose wealth would clearly be better spent elsewhere).[15]

Militarists would argue that Britain's vast military-industrial complex is needed to prevent attacks by terrorists, and to dissuade Russia from invading eastern Europe. This reasoning is circular. Militarism begets terrorism, which begets further militarism. Had NATO disbanded when the Soviet Union dissolved, instead of expanding inexorably towards Russia's western border, it's doubtful whether Russia would pose any kind of threat at all. Likewise, decades of Western interventions in the Middle East have left the region more unstable than ever, and posing a greater terrorist threat than ever before.

There is a second reason why Britain is much poorer than the rest of northern Europe – again, a reason that is rarely noted. For five years in a row, when many of today's retired people were children, tens of thousands of tonnes of explosives rained down on British cities. Most of the explosives were dropped from aeroplanes, some were delivered by rockets fired from France. In one instance, five people in Coventry were killed by a device planted by Irish republicans, who were colluding with the German war machine.

Europeans are not very good at contextualizing these events. They remain traumatic. Some people prefer to pretend that they occurred so long ago that they have no practical bearing on day-to-day life now. Although understandable, perhaps, this state of denial has clouded our understanding of the lasting economic consequences of warfare. Countries such as Britain and Germany would be much wealthier today if the two world wars had never happened.

To understand why, one need only take a walk around Coventry, an industrial city that was carpet-bombed by some 500 aeroplanes between 1940 and 1942. The damage to its medieval architecture was so great that almost all of it was bulldozed and replaced with grey, concrete structures that were built as cheaply as possible in the 1950s. In 2017, the city's authorities announced they would be spending £17 million in an attempt to upgrade the city centre to the original 1950s plans, which had proven unaffordable in the post-war austerity of the time.

Coventry is just one of many, many examples of costs from the Second World War that are falling on the current generation of taxpayers. One quarter of Britain's population was displaced by the conflict.[16] Re-housing them required the rapid, low-cost construction of residential projects, such as the brutalist Barbican Estate in London, which was built on a heavily bombed area. The Big City Plan to regenerate central Birmingham, another area hastily built after wartime devastation, is estimated to cost some £10 billion.[17]

After the war many schools and dwellings were assembled from pre-fabricated units that, unlike the brick and stone structures they replaced, could not last more than a few decades. The pre-fabricated bungalows of the Excalibur Estate in Catford, southeast London, were assembled by German and Italian prisoners of war in the 1940s, becoming the largest such estate in Europe. These shacks are still inhabited well into the 21st century, even though the housing is far below modern standards, according to the local authorities.[18]

There were less-visible costs. Many survivors of the two world wars had what we now call post-traumatic stress disorder (PTSD), which was known at the time as 'shell shock'. Such trauma can create unpleasant memories that are so vivid they seem more 'real' than the present moment. Veterans of the two conflicts had virtually no professional support to deal with their symptoms. Alcohol was prescribed by doctors to soldiers diagnosed with 'shell shock'.[19] Calculating the economic costs of PTSD in the decades since is difficult, but they are likely to be large, given the adverse effects that PTSD has on employability, domestic stability and the individual's general ability to function in society.

Other costs are highly visible. Britain only finished paying its billions of dollars-worth of Second World War debts to the US and Canada in 2006, after 61 years, and only settled its First World War debts in 2015, more than a century after that conflict began.[20] Germany's wartime debts were largely forgiven, but by the year 2000 it was nonetheless estimated to have paid almost $40 billion in wartime reparations.[21] Just as British cities such as Coventry and Plymouth needed to be rebuilt, so too did German cities such as Dresden, which had been levelled by British and American bombing raids.

But while Germany used aid money from the US Marshall Plan for reconstruction, Britain is widely perceived to have wasted its equivalent allocation – which was much larger than the German amount – on maintaining the vast military superstructure needed to police the British Empire. As Deputy Prime Minister Herbert Morrison put it in November 1949:

> '*We are in danger of paying more than we can afford for defences that are nevertheless inadequate, or even illusory.*'[22]

Had military expenditure been *subtracted* from the national accounts, rather than added to it, the wastefulness of this error would have been identified far more quickly. GDP is a calculation that counts money that is wasted as every bit as 'positive' as money that is invested. Reforming this absurd system, or at least raising awareness as to why it is so absurd, must be part of the core mission of the Departments for Peace.

The technical term for money spent on undesirable goods is 'defensive expenditures'. These cover military and police spending, but also things like cleaning up pollution, or air-conditioning units that are required to make life in a desert such as Arizona bearable for its inhabitants. To quote Professor Tim Jackson, an expert in sustainable development at the UK's University of Surrey:

> '*Since just after World War Two, we have relied on key economic indicators such as Gross Domestic Product (GDP), and recently Gross Value Added (GVA) to guide policy. However, as politicians from Robert Kennedy to David*

*Cameron to Jose Manuel Barroso have commented, these
indicators are not appropriate as measures of progress
or wellbeing: they conflate expenditure that improves our
wellbeing with defensive expenditure, they do not capture
our depreciation of economic capital, let alone our natural
or social ones, and they make crude assumptions about the
value of money and of economic activity. In short, we need
to move "beyond GDP".*[23]

Jackson is one of many thinkers who have sought to replace
GDP with something better, in his case the Regional Index of
Sustainable Economic Well-Being (R-ISEW). Sadly, none of
these attempts have gained traction with governments or the
media, who mulishly refuse to use anything other than GDP
as their synonym for what constitutes 'the economy'. Our
Departments for Peace must take the lead in ending this state
of affairs, in order to head off the twin disasters of military
and environmental apocalypse.

One reason that governments remain wedded to GDP is
because the calculation is so easy to rig. In February 2018,
the Trump administration announced an enormous $94
billion increase to the defence budget, taking it up to $700
billion – a rise of 15 per cent. It included defence programmes
the military had not even asked for, such as a 'space
force'.[24] Trump had no idea how he would pay for this: his
administration had also slashed taxes. The gap between taxes
and the things they were supposed to pay for, known as the
budget deficit, was expanding rapidly, but Trump didn't care.

A seasoned entrepreneur, Trump realized that the budget
deficit mess would be cleaned up by some other president in
the future. In the meantime, by splurging borrowed money
on the military, the result would – inevitably – be that US
GDP went up. All GDP does is count the money being spent.
Depressingly, Trump was proven right, with US growth
outstripping that of all the other advanced economies. 'The
world prepares itself for the Donald Trump boom' reported the

Financial Times in April 2018. In August the *Washington Post* concurred: 'Under Trump, the jobs boom has finally reached blue-collar workers.'

So long as reporters continue to conflate GDP growth with boomtime economic success, canny, unscrupulous politicians have an incentive to accelerate this doom-loop whereby they waste money they don't have on weapons they don't need. Tinkering around the edges will do nothing to change this: only by reforming the way GDP is calculated can this cycle be broken. Departments for Peace need to stop defensive expenditures being treated and reported as if they were the same kind of expenditure as weddings, soft furnishings and trips to the zoo.

One only need look at Switzerland to understand the economic benefits of avoiding this Trumpian doom-loop. At almost $40,000, the Swiss enjoy one of the highest average disposable incomes in the world – 33 per cent greater than that of the United Kingdom, according to OECD data.[25] Switzerland achieved this despite never having a global empire like Britain's, or even any access to maritime shipping, being a landlocked country.

Its mountainous terrain is not particularly conducive to agriculture or the building of transport infrastructure, unlike the fertile plains of England. Switzerland lacks Britain's oil reserves, its large domestic market, its monolingual culture and global profile. Moreover, it lacks a large standing military to buy its weapons, although Switzerland manages to export more arms per head than does the UK.[26]

But Switzerland enjoys one advantage over Britain that trumps all the UK's other strengths. The Swiss have enjoyed 200 years of unbroken peace. Their cities were never shattered by aerial bombardment or overrun by foreign soldiers, their workforce was never diverted away from productive endeavour to build weapons or wear uniform, their national psyche was never corrupted by dreams of militaristic grandeur or illusions of martial potency.

None of this is to say that Switzerland's neutrality against the genocidal Nazi war machine was entirely admirable, any more than one could argue it was wrong for most other European countries to fight the Nazis, at terrible cost to themselves. Although Switzerland accepted tens of thousands of Jewish refugees from the Holocaust, it also rejected tens of thousands, and it was a major market for artworks and other wealth stolen from victims of the genocide. In 1999 the Swiss government apologized to [the Jewish community] for their treatment.[27]

But on a narrowly economic level, Switzerland demonstrates the huge benefits of peace when it comes to material prosperity. If every European country had chosen to behave like the Swiss in 1914, to relinquish their imperial militarism and content themselves with life behind their own borders, then not only would many millions of lives have been saved, but Europe would be a vastly wealthier continent today than it actually is. In this sense, the mission of the Departments for Peace can be seen as Swissification.

1 'The US employment effects of military and domestic spending priorities: 2011 update', Pollin, Robert & Garrett-Peltier, Heidi, Political Economy Research Institute, University of Massachusetts, Amherst 2 Defence Diversification: International learning for Trident jobs, a research report by Nuclear Education Trust, June 2018, nin.tl/defence-diversification 3 Stanford Encyclopedia of Philosophy, 2017, 'Adam Smith's Moral and Political Philosophy', 27 January, plato.stanford.edu/entries/smith-moral-political 4 Huxley, Aldous, 1931, *A Brave New World*, Vintage, Penguin Random House, p 13 5 Newmont Mining, 'History of Newmont Mining', newmont.com/about-us/history/default.aspx 6 Lendon, Brad, 2018, 'What the massive US military budget pays for', CNN, 28 March, nin.tl/us-military-spending 7 DeVine, Michael E, 2018, 'Intelligence Community Spending: Trends and Issues, Congressional Research Service, 18 June, nin.tl/intel-spending 8 McCarthy, Niall, 2017, 'How Much Do U.S. Cities Spend Every Year On Policing? [Infographic]', Forbes, 7 August, nin.tl/us-spending-policing 9 Amaded, Kimberley, 2018, 'U.S. Military Budget, Its Components, Challenges, and Growth', The Balance, 4 September, nin.tl/us-budget 10 The World Bank, GDP indicator, nin.tl/gdp-indicator

11 OECD, 'As percentage of total adult population (aged 15 years and over), 2016 or nearest year'. **12** Scutti, Susan, 2017, 'Drinking water blamed in hundreds of illnesses, 13 deaths, CDC reports', CNN, 9 November, nin.tl/water-contamination **13** Eurostat, Gross domestic product (GDP) at current market prices by NUTS, two regions, nin.tl/eurostat-explorer **14** Eurostat, Government expenditure on defence, data extracted in March 2018, nin.tl/gov-expend **15** Macias, Amanda, 2018, 'The US spent $686 billion on defense last year – here's how the other NATO countries stack up', CNBC, 6 July, cnbc.com/2018/07/03/nato-spending-2017.html **16** 'Understanding post-war architecture', University of Leicester, nin.tl/pw-timeline **17** See Wikipedia, en.wikipedia.org/wiki/Big_City_Plan **18** See Wikipedia, en.wikipedia.org/wiki/Excalibur_Estate **19** Jones, Edgar and Fear, Nicola T, 2011, 'Alcohol use and misuse within the military: A review', International Review of Psychiatry, April 2011; 23: 166–172. **20** Cosgrave, Jenny, 2015, 'UK finally finishes paying for World War I', CNBC, 9 March, nin.tl/paying-wwi **21** Gibbs, Alexandra, 2015, 'Who still owes what for the two World Wars?', CNBC, 18 March, nin.tl/who-owes **22** Barnett, Corelli, 'The Wasting of Britain's Marshall Aid', BBC History, 2011, nin.tl/british-marshall **23** Jackson, Tim, Introduction to The Regional Index of Sustainable Economic Well-Being (R-ISEW), Centre for Well-Being, nef (the new economics foundation), UK, nin.tl/beyond-gdp **24** Burns, Robert, 2018, 'A Pentagon budget like none before: $700 billion', Associated Press, 11 February, nin.tl/pentagon-budget **25** OECD, 'Household disposable income, Gross adjusted, US dollars/capita', 2016, nin.tl/disposable-income **26** Jackson, Allison, 2014, 'Peace-loving Sweden and Switzerland are among top arms exporters per capita in the world', PRI, 23 May, nin.tl/peace-loving **27** BBC News, 1999, 'Swiss apology to Jewish refugees', BBC, 10 December, nin.tl/swiss-apology

Chapter 6

The Warmongers' Economy

An understanding of economics is not particularly useful for entrepreneurs in peace.

This is because economics, or at least economics as it is expressed by the Western media, has become one of the forces that propels humankind to war. It has mutated out of the social-science faculty to become a malign ideology that insists on environmental despoliation, competition rather than co-operation, and an ever-expanding military-industrial complex. Understanding the correct way to *reject* economics offers a valuable lesson in how impact investors and peace entrepreneurs can change the world for the better.

My 2012 book *The Economics of Killing* revealed the role played by the arms trade in the financial crisis of 2008. Summarized briefly, the trade in weapons had created an enormous trade mismatch between China and the US. Americans wished to buy the vast array of consumer goods produced in China and, in return, China wished to buy high-technology American products and companies, particularly those in the defence sector. The US government refused to allow this. As a result, the Chinese had little choice but to lend their hundreds of billions of surplus dollars back to the Americans, a line of ultra-cheap credit which inflated the asset bubbles that popped so spectacularly in 2008, delivering misery and crisis in their wake.

The book also noted the near-pathological refusal of Western economists to mention the role played by armaments in this imbalance. Their Chinese counterparts, by contrast, mentioned it frequently and continue to do so. As the country's Xinhua news agency reported in March 2018, a decade after the crisis:

> '*Another factor that has often been overlooked is that US control of high-tech exports to China contributed a lot to trade deficit with China, [Commerce] Minister Zhong said earlier this month, quoting one US research report which estimated a 35-per-cent fall in trade deficit with China if the United States relaxed export restrictions.*'[1]

In the years since *The Economics of Killing* was published, the problems created by this imbalance have become more acute, rather than less so. President Donald Trump has started a trade war with countries such as China and Germany, because they sell far more to Americans than they buy from them. Trump blames this for the de-industrialization of his country's midwestern heartlands and the hardship it has visited upon them.

At the same time, Trump has castigated Germany and other European nations for not spending the NATO-mandated two per cent of GDP on their armies, navies and air forces. Few if any commentators have pointed out the connection between the two issues.

Trump is demanding that countries such as Germany, although pledged to a peaceful existence, radically increase their spending on weapons systems. What goes unsaid is that Trump wants them to buy *American* weapons, with the US relying on arms exports to balance its trade. In 2017 the US defence sector generated a trade surplus of $86 billion, more than any other part of the American economy.[2] Balanced trade and militarized exports go hand in hand.

It should be little wonder, then, that in January 2018 Trump called for a 'whole of government' approach to pushing US arms sales overseas.[3] The President's own contribution has been to deliver an ultimatum to America's friends: buy our tanks, our warplanes and our missiles, or we will block your exports to the US.

Trump's actions have been universally condemned by Western economists. They insist that what they call 'free trade' is essential not only to prosperity, but also to world peace. Thus when in 2016 the UK's leader of the opposition, Jeremy Corbyn, referred to 'free trade dogma', he was attacked by members of other parties, and even by colleagues within his own Labour movement, as an enemy of the liberal world order.[4] However, when it comes to the relationship between trade and peace, Corbyn was in good company.

In 1933 John Maynard Keynes, one of Britain's greatest economists, gave a lecture in Ireland in which he dismissed the widespread assumption that free trade promotes the cause of peace. 'Take as an example the relations between England and Ireland,' Keynes offered. 'The fact that the economic interests of the two countries have been for generations closely intertwined has been no occasion or guarantee of peace.'[5] On the contrary, Keynes argued, friendship between Ireland and Britain would have been much easier were it not for the dense entanglement of their economic interests. Speaking 15 years after the end of the First World War, Keynes concluded:

> *'The age of economic internationalism was not particularly successful in avoiding war... I am inclined to the belief that, after the transition is accomplished, a greater measure of national self-sufficiency and economic isolation between countries, than existed in 1914, may tend to serve the cause of peace rather than otherwise.'*

Many historical and recent events support Keynes' view. The Opium Wars of the 1800s between Britain and China were triggered by the latter closing its markets to British opium, but that scarcely counts as a case in favour of free trade. It is much more persuasive that China should never have admitted Britain's opium traders in the first place.

More recently, the war between Russia and Ukraine that started in 2014 pitted against each other two countries with incredibly extensive trading links – trade that actually *grew* as the sides' soldiers were killing each other.[6] The once-prevalent belief that countries which both had McDonald's restaurants would never go to war had collapsed.

It is true that many thinkers believe that unfettered free trade prevents warfare. In their 2000 book *Triangulating Peace: Democracy, Interdependence, and International Organizations*, Ivy League political scientists Bruce Russett and John R Oneal laid out the argument for dense trading links reducing the scope for conflict. This so-called 'capitalist peace theory' is accepted unquestioningly by many commentators and intellectuals.

But to be beneficial for peace, free trade needs to be tightly regulated at an inter-governmental level, to ensure that common standards are applied. This was a point I made in my own 2016 book, *Peace Beyond Borders*. Free trade is possible within the European Union, for instance, because it creates common standards that are subject to democratic oversight by the European Parliament, and its member states agree on what constitutes a level playing field. What happens when such common standards are absent? The result is that free trade goes from being an economic truce to grounds for economic and even physical warfare.

In his 1997 book *Has Globalization Gone Too Far?*, Harvard trade economist Dani Rodrik showed that trade creates 'arbitrage' in national norms and social institutions.[7] In other words, it can trigger a race to the bottom in working conditions and environmental rules. Rodrik noted that in Europe, the EU acts to prevent this 'social dumping', but that there is no equivalent institution on a global scale. If a shoemaker in the US goes out of business because a shoemaker in Vietnam is technically more efficient and thus produces cheaper shoes, then fair enough. If the American company goes out of business because its Vietnamese rival uses child labour to cut payroll costs, that is another matter entirely.

Rodrik made similar observations about other forms of unfair trade, such as governments that use taxpayers' money to support particular industries, or countries where barriers to exports are more subtle than rules and tariffs. His book was read by President Bill Clinton, who drew upon it in his 1998 State of the Union address. Clinton pledged to triple the funding for American workers dislocated by globalization, and swore that the US would use its growing number of trade agreements to eliminate child labour. Twenty years later, it is clear that Clinton's approach did not succeed. Child labour is very much with us, as is the anger of blue-collar Americans over trade they perceive to be unfair. One does not need to admire Trump to realize that his critique of globalized trade is grounded in some uncomfortable and longstanding problems that have not been properly addressed.

Yet Trump's decision to pull away the rug, by imposing huge tariffs on exports from countries such as China and Germany, could bring catastrophe. China's ruling Communist Party relies on perpetual economic growth for legitimacy. In the event of a trade war, China's fragile financial system could easily collapse, given the country's reliance on export revenues and the vast number of hidden loans across its financial system. Facing such a crisis, the Communist Party may be tempted to do something many other governments have done throughout history: stage a diversionary war, to absorb the unemployed into the military and give them an external, rather than internal, enemy. This alarming scenario illustrates Keynes' dictum that the kind of dense economic relationship that exists between the US and China – countries with vastly different cultures and political systems – is a much greater risk to world peace than countries pursuing economic self-sufficiency.

This is just one example of why peace entrepreneurs should be suspicious of the standard economic arguments parroted too often in the media. Free trade does not prevent war. It might not even be economically beneficial, when taken to extremes. Rodrik, a longstanding dissenter from the free-trade consensus, cites the economic historian Paul Bairoch, when explaining why developing nations in 1900 produced only around half the quantity of manufactured goods they did in 1830:

> 'There cannot be any question but that the cause of de-industrialization in the [Global South] lay in the massive influx of European manufactured goods, especially textiles, on the markets of these countries.'[8]

Western countries are now tasting this effect for themselves – a major reason for their de-industrialization and the rise of men like Trump. Rodrik notes that the 'hyper-globalization' created by the World Trade Organization has had only a very small impact in improving overall output in Western countries, but that it has had a very large effect on the manufacturing sector, which in many cases has evaporated in the West. Nor, Rodrik notes, is there a political mechanism that readily allows the losers from this process – the desolate post-industrial towns of mid-western America or northern Britain – to be compensated by the winners. Trumpism and other radical movements have thrived in such areas as a direct response to this process of trade-induced de-industrialization. This thought should prompt further scepticism about the benign relationship between trade and peaceful coexistence.

Free trade is not the only example of media parroting the preferred line of big business. Likewise, journalists tend to assume that foreign investment is always beneficial to poor countries, and its withdrawal a disaster for them. This is not true either. As noted in the previous chapter, UNCTAD advice makes it clear that foreign investment is never the central plank of national peace or prosperity.

Peace entrepreneurs should bear this in mind when planning new enterprises. The talking-head economists who appear on rolling business news channels are for the most part private-sector 'economic consultants' whose fees are paid by powerful corporations, including in the defence sector. These economists have an unfortunate tendency to claim that policies which are good for their clients are also 'good for the economy'. Thus the West's economic narrative is driven not by the consistent application of economic theory, but by powerful conglomerates pushing their own agenda.

Such economists tell us, for instance, that mineral-rich African countries should open their markets to global mining giants such as Glencore and Rio Tinto. Local governments should clear out 'inefficient' and 'illegal' artisanal miners, who are invariably local Africans, so that the high-tech global giants can go about their business.

But where did the mining giants come from? In the US in the 1800s, the California Gold Rush transformed an impoverished wasteland into one of richest states in the union. This transformation was accomplished not by foreign transnationals but by amateur American miners who learnt on the job. Their activities brought roads, bridges and skilled artisans to California. California's Empire Mining Co. was set up during the gold rush, in 1854. In 1916 it was bought by a New York investment company called Newmont, which then became a mining company.[9] Today, Newmont Mining Corporation is one of the biggest in the world.

Yet the West's economic narrative is 'do as I say, not do as I did'. Big market players do not want 'new Newmonts' emerging from Africa, and their proxies in the Western media denigrate the work of artisanal African miners as dangerous, inefficient and polluting. Occasionally, the truth slips out, quietly. In January 2018, two World Bank economists, Victoire Girard and Remi Bazillier, published research showing that 'gold rush' style mining in Africa makes households in the surrounding area richer.[10] Industrial mining does not.

As a rule of thumb, peace activists seeking to assist fragile states and communities should take a leaf out of Keynes' book. They should aim to assist their self-sufficiency, and ensure that peace-enterprises empower and up-skill their local partners, transferring knowledge and giving them access to richer markets. Conversely, they should avoid merely 'opening up the local market' for big foreign players who are pursuing revenue growth.

Around the world, more than 220,000 people are classified as 'ultra-high net worth', with personal wealth of at least $30 million. Combined, their assets are worth a staggering $27 trillion, a sum about 50 per cent bigger than the US economy. All this, in the hands of a population smaller than that of Baltimore, Bristol, Bordeaux or Brisbane.

In the era of globalization, much of this wealth lies outside the reach of tax collectors, in a constellation of tax havens. National treasuries must content themselves with taxing the not-so-rich. In many European countries, even the poorest of the poor pay anything up to 25 per cent value-added tax on clothes, footwear, children's pushchairs, school uniforms, heating, electricity, hygiene products and a host of other essentials.

This state of affairs is provoking indignation on a global scale, as many of the so-called 'one percenters' are acutely aware. This indignation threatens the very fabric of liberal democracy, the political system on which many of their fortunes depend, producing a populist wave that seeks enemies within and without. For all the faults of liberal democracy, it is not clear that the revolutions to replace it would produce a better one.

This presents peace activists with an opportunity, and a responsibility. In order to preserve the basis of the system that sustains them, the 'one percenters' must demonstrate that they are giving something back. By working with them, peace activists can mobilize their wealth to heal some of the social divisions that lead to conflict, allowing the 'one per cent' to demonstrate that they are not wholly self-interested.

The election of Trump, the UK's decision to exit the European Union, the dizzying rise of extremist political parties in continental Europe, and the profusion of 'strongman' leaders worldwide should be enough to warn the 'one per cent' that the clock is ticking on their preferred, liberal, 'hands off' systems of national and international government. As expressed memorably by Mark Blyth, a British politics professor at Brown University on Rhode Island, New York, the Hamptons are not a defensible position. Wealth and expensive neighbourhoods offer no protection against the social and political conflict engendered by the current socio-economic system.

Peace entrepreneurs should have no qualms whatsoever in approaching such high-net-worth individuals for financial support. They know, as we know, that evolutions are always preferable to revolutions, which often dispense not only with the bathwater of social injustice, but also with the baby that is public security and welfare. Creating a socially just economy is in the interests of the very poor, but also of the very rich.

Beyond that, a new system of measuring prosperity is urgently needed. Not only do we need to end the absurdity wherein activities that are actively destructive are counted as part of GDP, and thus 'growth', but we also need to insist that constructive activities, which are often voluntary, are included in the national accounts.

The cost of the police and prison service is counted in GDP, but GDP ignores the work of the parents, grandparents, volunteers and other unpaid carers and mentors who raise children into peaceable, law-abiding adults. Until GDP is reformed into something that reflects good works, rather than ignoring them, it is beholden on peace activists to regard the conventional economic narrative surrounding growth, trade and investment with more than a pinch of salt.

If we look into the future, the revolution in automation and technology will make millions of people redundant, a huge economic concern. The sense of who we are and what we gain from work is an important part of our identity. How will humanity cope with such huge unemployment which could threaten the stability of societies and trigger unrest? Our hope is in the inventiveness and flexibility of future human beings who will harness the power of technology, critical thinking and creativity, and willingness to work together to solve future challenges and forge a common sustainable future for all, sharing the finite resources of our planet equitably in a peaceful and compassionate way.

---

1 Xinhua, 2018, 'Truth behind China-US trade "imbalances"', 27 March, nin.tl/xinhua **2** Cebul, Daniel, 2018, 'US leads the world in 2017 aerospace and defense exports say AIA report', Defense News, 12 February, nin.tl/us-aeropsace **3** Stone, Mike and Spetalnick, Matt, 2018, 'Trump to call on Pentagon, diplomats to play bigger arms sales role – sources', Reuters, 8 January. **4** Blanchard, Jake, 2016, 'Jeremy Corbyn wants Britain to abandon membership of EU single market, sources say', Mirror, 7 September, nin.tl/corbyn-abandon **5** Keynes, John Maynard, 1933, 'National Self-Sufficiency', *The Yale Review*, Volume 22, no. 4, pp 755-769. **6** Peterson, Nolan, 2018, 'Long at war with each other, Ukraine and Russia trade on,' Newsweek, 28 January, nin.tl/ukraine-russia **7** Rodrik, Dani, 1997, 'Tensions Between Trade and Domestic Social Arrangements', *Has Globalization Gone Too Far?*, Institute for International Economics, Chapter 3. **8** Rodrik, Dani, 2012, *The Globalisation Paradox: Why Global Markets, States and Democracy Can't Coexist*, Oxford University Press, p 141. **9** Newmont Mining, 'History of Newmont Mining', newmont.com/about-us/history/default.aspx **10** Lendon, Brad, 2018, 'What the massive US military budget pays for', CNN, 28 March, nin.tl/us-military-spending

PART 2

THE WORLD AS IT IS – EVER MORE DANGEROUS

Chapter 7

Bullets That Think

My 2016 book *Peace Beyond Borders* ended with a troubling postscript.[1]

It highlighted a 2009 presentation given by the US Department of Defense, which revealed that the US Air Force is considering the use of tiny flying devices to conduct what, in the words of its author General David Deptula, would be 'indoor lethal' operations. In other words, these tiny mechanical insects would become like bullets that never miss, buzzing into the victims to discharge a fatal payload of poison or explosives.

The postscript described the huge investments already being made into such systems. Such tiny drones wold be used individually, but also in 'swarms' that would see thousands of them tasked with eliminating human adversaries *en masse*.

Since *Peace Beyond Borders* was published, a seven-minute video has been posted on YouTube that should be required viewing for every peace activist. Entitled 'Slaughterbots', it dramatizes the way such micro-drones will be used in the future – as a means to conduct assassinations with little to no risk on the part of the assassin, in a way that could effectively shut down all forms of dissent.[2] How can anyone ever be truly safe, if a tiny and virtually undetectable aircraft can be used to kill?

Our only guarantee is that these technologies will become rapidly more capable and widespread. DARPA, the US defence research agency, had swarms of nano-quadcopters flying in sequence over five years ago. Today, it has a drone that can navigate indoors at speeds of over 70 km/h (45 mph), far too fast for a human to evade.[3] But China is catching up. In June 2017 its CTEC corporation launched a swarm of

119 micro-drones, breaking the US Air Force's record of 103 set only a few months previously, which were launched from Boeing F/A-18 Super Hornet fighter jets.

Visualize a future in which the US and China go to war over the rocky islets in the South China Sea, claimed by China but also by much nearer countries such as Vietnam. Perhaps this will be the result of a trade war, as discussed earlier. A US aircraft carrier group approaches the Scarborough Shoal, carrying at least 7,500 personnel in at least four ships, with a nuclear submarine lurking somewhere beneath. Facing this armada is a single Chinese destroyer, armed only with racks upon racks of tiny, unmanned aerial vehicles (UAVs).

Yet once deployed, the UAVs quickly overpower the American warships. They target the fighters on the aircraft carrier deck, shattering their canopies and rendering them unflyable. They ram the ships' radar arrays, destroying their ability to survey the surrounding area and target their missile systems. Beneath the waves, submersible drones lock on to the sound emitted by the submarine's propellers and then immobilize them with explosives. The carrier group's conventional strength is no more effective than would be that of a bear attacked by a swarm of angry bees.

The technology makes sense for China's military. It is attempting to level the playing field with the US, which has a huge advantage in conventional weaponry and experience, and which spends four times the amount on its military than the Chinese do on theirs, as part of Washington's wasteful financial support for the corporate 'welfare queens' of the defence sector. Mass-produced micro-drones, in many ways similar to the Chinese-made toys already found in many households, but exploiting adaptive algorithms that can give them autonomy on the battlefield, are what pass for a logical choice in the demented world of the military industry. A cheap short-cut that could save them hundreds of billions of dollars, while threatening billions of lives.

As if this equation were not sufficiently alarming, one must add to the calculation the concept of artificial intelligence (AI). The world has grown accustomed to missiles that can lock on to an opponent's radar or heat signature, using this to track and then destroy its target. Humanity is much less prepared for weapons that could measure the contours of a target's silhouette in order to decide whether to destroy it, or the contours of a human face.

Committees before the UK's House of Lords are not known for lurching into science fiction. Britain's upper chamber is populated by unelected experts and political specialists whose job it is to review and revise legislation. Committee hearings are often a little dry. Yet one such committee on 30 November 2017 heard evidence that resembled a nightmarish Hollywood script.

The subject was AI. Even though such committee hearings are open to the public, this fascinating subject drew a sparse attendance – there were many more lords present than 'commoners'. Speaking first was Professor Chris Hankin, co-director of the Institute of Security Science and Technology at Imperial College, London.

Hankin noted that the US is developing automatic defensive systems, programs that can understand when they are under attack and repair themselves. In 10 to 15 years, he suggested, such technology would be elevated to the level of systems. His assessment was endorsed by Dr Mark Briers, Strategic Programme Director for Defence and Security at the Alan Turing Institute, who said that AI – specifically machine-learning – was already being deployed in the defence industry.

Briers said that within the next five to ten years, corporations and governments are likely to find their systems being attacked by artificially intelligent computer viruses. These, he said, are most likely to emerge from the state-sponsored sector, rather than from freelance hackers working alone, but the latter would gain access to them as the technology became democratized.

Next came Alvin Wilby, the Vice-President of Research at Thales, a giant French arms contractor that, he said, is a leading supplier of autonomous systems. It is reasonable to assume that in his professional capacity, Wilby has a greater knowledge of the pace and trajectory of weapons development than does the public at large. His warning was stark.

He noted that the Israelis have an aerial weapons system called Harpy which autonomously selects targets; it is capable of loitering over an area and then deciding which target to destroy – in theory only radar systems. The Harpy has been sold to several other countries, including China, a fact that so concerns the US government that in 2005 it demanded that Israel seize the Harpies it had sold to China, which had briefly been returned to Israel for an upgrade. The Israelis refused.

Wilby noted that the Russians have anti-submarine mines that can autonomously select targets. Alongside the threat of AI, he also highlighted the problem of 'artificial stupidity'; that such weapons would malfunction and target the 'wrong people'. He drew an analogy with another fast-emerging technology that must make life-and-death choices: 'If a self-driving car has been programmed to kill civilians, it's a lethal autonomous weapons system.'

Wilby said it was an 'absolute certainty' that rogue states and terrorists would utilize these new technologies in the very near future. A drone attack in 2015, he noted, tried to deliver radioactive sand to the Prime Minister of Japan's office. The technological challenge of scaling drones up to swarms does not require any huge inventive step, he noted. He also highlighted the StuxNet cyber-attack on Iran, which he said demonstrated some elements of AI.

Finally, and most cogently of all, Professor Noel Sharkey, a computer scientist and ethicist who was also testifying, asked why investment in AI wasn't being directed towards peaceful uses such as mine-clearance operations. He questioned whether the UK's declared ban on autonomous weapons was in fact meaningless, because it had set the bar for what qualifies as autonomy so high, to include oblique facets such as self-awareness and intention, that the ban was not really a ban at all.

Sharkey noted that British defence contractor BAE Systems is already testing the Taranis unmanned warplane and the small Ironclad unmanned tank, but that Britain was already a long way behind the US, which has unmanned fighter jets and submarines, and Russia, which has the T-14 Armata 'super-tank' equipped with an unmanned turret. The Russians are trying to make the tank fully autonomous as soon as possible.

'We are already seeing the beginnings of an arms race, which is why it's urgent to prevent this happening,' he added. 'Because once the genie's out of the bottle, then you've had it.' The Russian Kalashnikov neural network targeting system was 'certainly' fully autonomous, he said. 'People want autonomy because they say the battlefield is getting too fast for humans. I would say, let's slow down a bit... I don't want to live in a world where a war can happen in a few seconds accidentally.'

Speed is increasingly the watchword of the US Navy as it seeks to defend its vessels from the kind of drone attack described above. One of the fastest weapons on the planet is installed at a US Navy facility in Dahlgren, Virginia; an electromagnetic railgun that can fire projectiles at 4,500 mph (7,240 km/h) over a distance of 100 miles (161 kilometres), and which is planned for use on US surface vessels. But an even faster weapon has already found its way onto the *USS Ponce*, an amphibious transport ship.

It is equipped with a LaWS laser cannon designed to destroy aerial drones, small attack boats and incoming missiles. The electricity for each shot costs little more than a dollar, and the laser is both silent and invisible. However, LaWS would be unable to destroy an incoming swarm of drones unless its targeting system was controlled not by humans, but by AI algorithms operating at superhuman speeds to identify and destroy targets.

This raises the possibility that the wars of the future will be decided not by who has the most powerful gun or missile, but by whoever has the most powerful AI. In December 2017, Google's AlphaZero AI was given the basic rules of chess. With no further input, it learnt the game within four hours and then proceeded to beat the chess world champion – another computer program called Stockfish 8 – over the course of 100 games in which it did not lose a single one.

At the moment, AI specialists seeking to downplay fears over such AI systems point out that chess, unlike real life, is a closed system with a very large but nonetheless finite number of moves, a game that thus renders itself susceptible to brute-force number-crunching. There is an enormous difference between an AI being unable to understand board games such as chess and the Japanese game Go, they would argue, and comprehending the infinite complexity of existence on Planet Earth.

Yet herein lies one of the greatest reasons to fear AI. Just as humans and animals simplify their understanding of reality to prioritize those aspects that are most important to their everyday needs, so AI will inevitably reduce its understanding of reality to whatever purpose its creators have in mind.

A drone loitering over a conflict zone might use a microphone to detect humans speaking Arabic or Chinese, while ignoring those speaking English or French. It might then measure their height to avoid attacking children, or match the colours of their clothing to its database of military uniforms. Having identified its targets, it might then only attack them with tranquilizers or other non-lethal weapons.

Indeed, this seductive promise of non-lethal robot warfare is one reason the technology is potentially so dangerous. One group of people could invade and repress another with AI-directed machines without producing the overt bloodshed that typically draws a reaction from other countries and civilian protesters. 'The one who becomes leader in this will become ruler of the world,' Russia's President Vladimir Putin told a group of students in August 2016. Months earlier, a report by Harvard University suggested that an AI arms race was 'inevitable' and would be as revolutionary as the invention of nuclear weapons.

Putin was only one of a number of notable figures to warn of the dangers of AI. In August 2017, the tech entrepreneur Elon Musk, who is working on self-driving vehicles, warned on Twitter: 'If you're not concerned about AI safety, you should be. Vastly more risk than North Korea.' He said its development should be closely regulated. In November that year the astrophysicist Stephen Hawking also said that AI will become a 'new form of life that will outperform humans', adding: 'If people design computer viruses, someone will design AI that improves and replicates itself.'

Two years earlier both Hawking and Musk had signed an open letter calling for greater research into the societal impact of AI. It highlighted the point made by Wilby: that self-driving vehicles, for instance, would be required to make 'lesser of two evil' decisions in the event of sudden accidents, for instance whether to drive into another vehicle or onto the pavement – potentially, the difference between killing civilians and killing the driver. In the longer term, the letter worried about the rise of 'super intelligences' that do not act in accordance with human wishes.

To understand the power of AI, consider the ImageNet challenge. ImageNet is a library of some 10 million images, each labelled on a database. A fruit bowl, say, or a tiger. When the challenge started in 2010, the best image-recognition programs were mis-identifying a quarter of the objects in the pictures. Seven years later, amid rapid advances in AI, the error rate had fallen to below three per cent – better than humans. Another example is Google Translate. Today, this translation software uses neural-networks, which emulate the functioning of a brain, to translate not single words but rather to appreciate the meaning of entire sentences, vastly improving the translations.

Such technologies placed in the hands of governments raise some profound concerns. Deep-learning algorithms with access to internet records are able to identify users whose search activity is indicative of radicalization. In a perfect democracy, this could be a tool to prevent terrorist attacks. In the real world, it will be a valuable tool for dictators. In June 2017, the BBC revealed that BAe Systems had sold mass surveillance technology to the governments of Saudi Arabia, the UAE, Oman, Qatar, Algeria and Morocco that allowed them to monitor the mobile phone and internet use of their citizens, and even to track their locations.[4]

Even in democracies, one might worry that elected presidents will use such systems to limit opposition and, ultimately, turn elections into hollow exercises with no means of ousting an entrenched elite. The criminalization of free speech under the auspices of preventing antisemitism, xenophobia and 'fake news' could become the cover for a more insidious curtailment of public discourse. In April 2018 a man wanted for 'economic crimes' was identified by facial recognition cameras in a concert audience of 60,000 in Nanchang, China, and arrested by police.[5]

As such surveillance systems become more widespread, so too will cyber-attacks against them. The Anonymous collective of hackers has staged a series of cyber-intrusions against governments accused of human rights abuses. As AI algorithms bleed into the public domain, it is only a matter of time before such groups use AI-enabled malware to maximize the amount of damage their attacks can do. It raises the possibility of AI-enabled malware that can protect itself from deletion, for instance by changing its form to hide from anti-virus software. A Virginia-based company called Endgame is actively creating such malware, in order to develop defences against it.[6]

Cyber-crime is likely to evolve in tandem with technology. Criminals and terrorists could, for instance, use image-recognition to search the internet for individuals with whom they share a facial resemblance, and then target them for identity theft. This, for instance, may allow them to bypass the facial recognition technology that is now being used at airports.

However, fully weaponizing artificially intelligent software is likely to require the power of the state. Already, countries such as the US, Israel, Russia and China have military cyber-warfare commands. Ultimately, their goal will be to seize control of an enemy country's systems and turn their own weapons against them. In this scenario the Chinese destroyer's drones, rather than intercepting the American fleet, will turn back to target their own mothership.

All this is easily foreseeable as of 2019. However, so rapid is the pace of technological change that it is safe to assume the landscape will look very different come 2029, and different again in 2039. By that point, it is possible that concepts such as self-awareness might be facets of AI systems, raising profound philosophical and ethical questions around the nature of consciousness.

At that point, the possibility of an all-new enemy arises; that an artificial military intelligence, endowed with a sense of its own existence and a contextual understanding of current affairs, concludes that the greatest threat to the planet is humanity itself. There is very little indication that humanity is prepared for such a 'Terminator'-style turn of events, and every indication that the range of weapons that would be available to such an entity, ranging from nuclear weapons to swarms of tiny quadcopters, would be enough to eradicate billions of people.

What can be done? The role of peace activists is pivotal, as shown by the 'Slaughterbots' video, a joint project between University of California academic Stuart Russell and the Future of Life Institute, a volunteer organization based in Boston, Massachusetts. By using the power of YouTube to dramatize warnings about micro-drone technology, they were able to achieve over two million views within a couple of months.

Every new military development in the arena of drones and autonomous machines must be flagged to the general public, loudly and clearly, using not only documentary formats but also dramatic media. Letters to legislators are important, particularly those being lobbied by the defence industry, to demand greater scrutiny of defence contractors and their research and development processes. Activists should consider forming new movements dedicated to drone warfare activism, or AI activism, and should forge links with concerned journalists. Campaign management is critical.

Only through these means can we avoid 'boiling frog' syndrome, whereby the public comes to view innovations they once would have considered horrifying as merely part of a 'New Normal'. As workers for peace, this has always been among the main challenges we've faced, but with the rapidity of technological change in the 21st century, the stakes have never been higher.

---

1 Vijay Mehta's last book *Peace Beyond Borders: How the EU brought peace to Europe and how exporting it would end conflicts around the world* was published in 2016 in print and ebook (both £9.99) by New Internationalist, with a foreword written by Jose Ramos-Horta, Nobel Peace Laureate and former president of Timor-Leste. The book can be purchased online from europeforpeace.org.uk or from Amazon, Kobo, ePub, Apple iBooks and others. 2 Stop Autonomous Weapons, 2017, 'Slaughterbots', 12 November, nin.tl/slaughterbots 3 GeoBeats News, 2017, 'DARPA Video Shows Its New Drone Flying At 45 MPH Inside Warehouse', 14 February, nin.tl/darpa-drone 4 BBC, 2017, 'How BAE sold cyber-surveillance tools to Arab states', 15 June, bbc.co.uk/news/world-middle-east-40276568 5 BBC, 2018, 'Chinese man caught by facial recognition at pop concert', 13 April, bbc.co.uk/news/world-asia-china-43751276 6 Endgame, 2016, 'Domain Expertise And AI: Conquering The Next Generation Of Cyber Threats', 8 September, nin.tl/domain-ai

Chapter 8

The Clock Ticking to World War Three

Homo sapiens, as our species is known, has existed for at least 300,000 years. Some form of humanity has existed for much longer than that. What we call civilization, though, has been present for only a small fraction of that time, perhaps six millennia.

In other words, humans have been civilized for only two per cent of the time we have existed on this planet, at most. The other 98 per cent of human history is shrouded in the darkness of our uncivilized past. Perhaps because we know so little about our lives in that time, humanity has a tendency to pretend that this vast expanse of time does not matter, and that from it we sprang fully formed as the builders of towns and churches, the writers of sagas, the founders of states and growers of grain.

But rationally, it must be the case that even today, our human instincts are geared to that immense epoch that lies beyond the gaze of historians; that beneath our veneer of civilized existence lies the same animating forces that propelled humanity through aeons without electricity, without effective medicine, without writing or numbers, without roads or wheels, with little more than the bonds of family and whatever clothes and tools that could be hewn from the immediate environment.

This thought should strike us with a degree of fear.

We are not so different from the humans who, in their prehistory, murdered two per cent of their own population on average each year. This was six times the rate that other mammals kill each other, according to a 2016 paper led by

Dr José María Gómez of Granada University in Spain.[1] We are certainly not so different from the human beings who have killed each other *en masse* in the thousands of centuries since then.

Those humans were not equipped with a destructive toolkit that can obliterate entire cities at a stroke, or poison tens of thousands of people. Our destructive power has evolved exponentially more quickly than we have ourselves. It would not be wrong to say that cavemen are now in control of nuclear weapons, for we are not very different from cavemen.

Perhaps the only innovation that protects modern humans from ourselves is our ability to build institutions. Institutions are ways of interacting that do not die with their initiators, but rather are structured so they can be passed down through generation after generation. Institutions can be founded to limit our caveman tendency for annihilation.

The most alarming aspect of the current world is the way that our peaceful institutions have been sabotaged in the space of just 20 years. The most visible casualty has been the United Nations. Established after the devastation of the Second World War, for three generations it provided the institutional underpinnings of world peace, even as the superpower rivalry between communism and capitalism threatened nuclear oblivion.

The UN envisaged a world of sovereign states, each with their own UN representation in New York, their own sacrosanct borders, currencies and systems of self-determination. Many of these nation-states would be carved from the European empires of the pre-war era. The Belgian empire would give birth to countries such as Rwanda and the Democratic Republic of Congo (DRC); the Dutch empire would spawn the likes of Indonesia and Suriname; the Portuguese empire would yield Angola and Mozambique. These nation-states would then make their own way in the world, while the old colonial European powers would unite into a European Union, as a consolation for giving up imperial power.

The new international system was imperfect. There were many successes among the newly independent countries – the Singapores, Botswanas, Omans, the Trinidads and Senegals, the Indias, Malaysias, Jordans, Thailands and Maltas – but there were other countries that slipped into civil war, dictatorship and even greater poverty: the DRCs, the Sudans, the Yemens and the Afghanistans.

Rome could not be built in a day. Once, policymakers realized that the failures of the international system did not justify tearing down the whole edifice. For all its many faults, the UN Security Council was effective in preventing powerful countries from invading and subjugating weaker ones, and this mattered. When Iraq invaded the sovereign nation of Kuwait in 1990, the Security Council voted unanimously for a military intervention to expel the Iraqi invaders.

Once the Iraqis were driven out, the war ended. Like Kuwait's, the borders of Iraq were enshrined in international law. The UN Security Council resolution that authorized the Gulf War did not allow for invasion or 'regime change', notwithstanding the appalling human rights violations of Saddam Hussein's government. In those days, the leaders of France, America, China, Britain and the Soviet Union understood that they had no power to build a perfect world through military force, and that the best they could achieve were the stable, lawful, predictable institutions of the international system.

Alas, the end of the Cold War saw the rise of a new generation of leaders who did not recognize this limitation on their powers. They saw the defeat of Soviet communism as a green light to deliver liberal democracy at the point of a gun. The nation-state and the international system were out of date. The 'good guys' would no longer allow something as trivial as international borders and laws to circumscribe their ideology.

The first real blow was struck in 1999. That year, the Americans and their British allies bombed Yugoslavia, a federal republic that had slipped into civil war when one of its constituent states, Slovenia, decided its future lay inside a European Union rather than a pan-Slavic one. The unravelling of the Yugoslav federation created a sinister new expression, 'ethnic cleansing', to describe the inter-communal massacres that followed.

The Anglo-American bombing campaign was the first NATO operation to be conducted without the permission of the UN Security Council. It humiliated Russia and its then-president Boris Yeltsin; Serbia, the target of the aerial attacks, was a Russian ally. 'I told NATO, the Americans, the Germans, don't push us towards military action,' Yeltsin warned in April 1999. 'Otherwise there will be a European war for sure and possibly world war.'

There wasn't, at least not yet. Yeltsin resigned at the end of 1999. He handed over to his prime minister, Vladimir Putin.

The Yugoslav precedent led to the rapid unravelling of the Security Council's power. Borders began to be trampled with impunity. The US and a small number of its allies invaded Iraq in 2003, without authorization from the UN Security Council and with indifference to the protests in Britain, France, Germany and Russia. Five years later, war would return to Europe, as Russia invaded areas of neighbouring Georgia, again without reference to the UN.

In 2011, as the 'Arab Spring' uprisings swept North Africa, France, Britain and the United States ignored Russian objections and translated a limited UN mandate for air strikes in Libya into fully fledged regime change. This would plunge Libya into years of civil conflict and trigger a refugee crisis, redolent of the aftermath of the Iraq invasion.

Not to be outdone, in 2014 the Russian army annexed vast tracts of Ukraine, its neighbour to the west, as part of a strategic competition with the EU and US. The same year, the US and its allies would begin military action in Syria, which like Libya had been overcome by the 'Arab Spring' uprisings and overrun by civil war. By 2017 this military intervention escalated into US cruise missile attacks on Syrian government positions, again unauthorized by the UN. The year 2018 recorded the first direct military exchange between US and Russian forces in Syria. This was exactly the world-ending scenario that so much institutional energy had been committed to avoid since the end of the Second World War.

Within two decades, the institutions that had kept humankind from the brink of nuclear devastation had effectively collapsed. The UN system had given way to anarchy. There had been no meaningful reduction in the nuclear arsenals ranged across the world's continents. On the contrary, more and more countries had concluded that, in this lawless environment created by presidents Clinton, Putin and Bush, their hopes of preserving national self-determination rested on developing their own nuclear deterrents.

Countries like Pakistan, Iran and North Korea watched the unfolding situation and concluded that their best defence lay in nuclear offence. The Libyan civil war was a particularly vivid illustration of why they might conclude this. Libya had peacefully relinquished its nuclear programme in 2003, alongside its other weapons of mass destruction. This did nothing to save it from 'regime change', nor the horrors that came afterwards.

The seriousness of the situation required a serious response. Instead, some of the leading Western democracies embarked on a series of outlandish political experiments. In 2016 the US elected Donald Trump as president, a reality television personality and hotel developer known for his brash personality and irascible temper, who had never served in political office. That same year, Britain voted to exit the EU, a body dedicated to preserving peace in Western Europe, distracting European democracies from the perilous situation unfolding to their east.

In Russia, meanwhile, Putin has been in charge for longer than any Soviet leader except Stalin. He has no clear successor, and is rumoured to have amassed enormous personal wealth during his time in office.[2] He appears to have no intention of standing down, and has no serious political rival. Such attributes do not normally contribute to improved decision-making, the longer a leader remains in power.

Putin's Russia can no longer compete with the US in terms of military spending. The US defence budget has reached $700 billion a year, the equivalent of Argentina's entire economy. This is almost three times as much as is being spent by its closest competitor, China. Between them, the countries with the 25 biggest defence budgets spend $1.5 trillion every year preparing for war. The US is more than one third of that total.

This asymmetry makes nuclear weapons all the more appealing to weaker states. With no conceivable hope of matching the US in terms of conventional forces or expenditure, nuclear weapons have become a form of insurance against invasion. For a financial outlay that, though still ruinous for taxpayers, is cheaper than trying to match the US tank for tank, they can neutralize the vast might of the American military by acquiring weapons so indiscriminately devastating that the US would not dare invade.

The destruction of the UN-based international system has solved no problems. Global democracy did not flourish as a result of Clinton, Bush, Putin, France's Nicolas Sarkozy and Britain's Tony Blair sidelining the UN. The US, Russia, Iran and many other players continue to organize and finance proxy wars in countries such as Syria and Yemen, just as they did during the Cold War. It was never difficult to imagine the proxy war being fought between US and Russian-backed fighters in Syria mushrooming into a direct conflict between Russian and American service personnel, with casualties on both sides. Nor is it difficult to conceive of a bungled US raid on North Korea escalating into a conflict in which nuclear weapons are used. These are doomsday scenarios.

North Korea has voiced its intention to develop nuclear missiles capable of striking the US mainland. Until it has demonstrated such a capability, it remains at risk of a pre-emptive attack by the US military from its bases in South Korea and Japan. The US is unlikely to request UN Security Council clearance for such an invasion because China, one of the North's few allies, would veto it, as might Russia.

The other military options are scarcely any better. Rumours that emanated from Washington DC in early 2018 suggested that Trump was contemplating a 'bloody nose' operation against North Korea, whereby the US would fire missiles at some of North Korea's military or nuclear installations, or have aircraft drop bombs on them, as a sign of US resolve. These rumours arose after the head of the CIA claimed it would only be a 'handful of months' before North Korea could strike the US mainland with a nuclear weapon.

To his credit, Trump then attempted to negotiate with Pyongyang, a difficult enterprise for even the most adept diplomatic mind. His quixotic peace overtures towards the North, even were they successful, were likely in practice simply to reset the situation to that of the 1990s, when the North would use bilateral talks with the Clinton administration to extract cash for its senior regime figures, in exchange for suspending (but not ending) its nuclear programme. While much better than war, this would never be a durable solution.

Either scenario would likely only succeed in persuading China to drop its already half-hearted economic sanctions against the North. If tensions were to persist, North Korea has already developed the means to retaliate via asymmetrical means, whether they be cyber-attacks, assassinations and other acts of terrorism, or submarine strikes on South Korean warships or merchant vessels.

---

1 Gómez, José María et al, 2016, 'The phylogenetic roots of human lethal violence', *Nature*, issue 558, 12 October, pp 233-237, nature.com/articles/nature19758- **2** Zhdannikov, Dmitry, 2014, 'What does U.S. know about Putin's oil wealth?', Reuters, 21 March, nin.tl/putin-oil-wealth

Chapter 9

The War on Nature

In 2017, 35 billion barrels of crude oil were drilled from the ground and from beneath the sea, each barrel containing some 160 litres, of thick, bituminous liquid.[1] To store it all in one location would require a container that was five kilometres long, five kilometres wide and five kilometres tall. Such a tank would need to be installed in an area twice the size of Manhattan's Central Park, and would be six times taller than the Burj tower in Dubai, the world's tallest skyscraper.

In 2017, humankind dug up over seven billion tonnes of coal.[2] Laid out in a single row, this coal would rise as a range of hills stretching from the city of New York to the shores of Lake Michigan.

In 2017, 3.7 trillion cubic metres of natural gas was extracted from the ground.[3] This was enough to fill 17 million airships the size of the giant Hindenburg Zeppelin that crashed in 1937.

Imagine for a moment what would happen were this a mountain range, and those millions of airships, and this giant oil tank to be arrayed in the eastern US. The oil tank mounted on Central Park and the Upper East Side, the mountain range of coal stretching from New York City to the Midwest, the Zeppelins parked along the way.

What if someone set all this ablaze?

The ensuing ecological catastrophe would force the evacuation of a dozen states. The health effects of inhaling the air within 1,000 miles of the blaze would render the region uninhabitable. New York would be irrecoverable. Millions would die.

Yet on a global scale, this is precisely what humanity does with every passing year. With every passing year, the coal mountains become larger, the oil lake more voluminous and the airships more plentiful. Each year, humankind burns billions of tonnes of biomass such as wood and foliage for heat and light. In this way, humans emit 45 times more carbon dioxide than all the volcanic eruptions on earth.[4]

A very large majority of scientists believe that our continuous burning of fossil fuel is changing our planet's climate. The greatest suffering is likely to fall on countries where survival is already difficult – those places where farmers eke out crops on the edges of deserts, where the water table underground is already too drained to support the people above, and where water wars will follow.

Dr Rajendra Singh, known as the 'water man of India', said in an interview with Amrita Gupta of the Carnegie Council:

> '*The Third World War is at our gate, and it will be about water, if we don't do something about this crisis. So many people in the Middle East and African countries are moving to places like Europe, in part because of water scarcity – after forced migration comes tension, conflict and terrorism. Where terrorism is active, there is usually a scarcity of water. Look at Syria – a long time ago, it had very good agriculture, but then Turkey built a dam that changed things. It's a similar story with Libya. If we want a safe future, we need to start harvesting and conserving water.*'[5]

He also said that in poor countries with severely water-stressed areas, community-based water harvesting and water-management initiatives are the best solutions, owing to lack of funds to buy, latest renewable technologies and infrastructure to harness sources of water.[5]

The only option for people facing droughts and floods in increasing frequency will be to migrate *en masse* to countries that are less severely affected. It is possible that this great migration has already begun. As migrants risk their lives crossing the Mediterranean to southern Europe, or traversing the Sonoran Desert in a bid to reach the US, they are dismissed in the West not as true refugees from war or persecution, but as mere 'economic migrants' fleeing poverty.

The potential for conflict should be clear to all concerned. In the West, such migrants are often traduced as little more than benefit scroungers who are willing to risk their children's lives for a chance at the easy life in temperate Europe or the US, whereas those displaced blame Europe and the US for the polluting emissions that made their lives unbearable. There is an academic consensus that the carbon footprints of inhabitants in wealthy countries are vastly larger than those of people in the poorest ones.

It is reasonable to suppose that there will be no such consensus on the relationship between climate change and conflict, or on what the main perpetrators of global warming owe to its victims. Proving beyond doubt the relationship between cause and effect is one of the hardest tasks in science. For centuries, scientists believed that the Black Death that devastated Europe in the 14th century was spread by rats' fleas. In recent years, however, the weight of scientific evidence has shifted, suggesting the main vector for infection was coughing and sneezing – a pneumonic, rather than bubonic, plague.[6]

Establishing the causes of a plague is simple compared to identifying the causal relationships between the activities of seven billion human beings and the atmosphere of a planet of 500 million square kilometres, and then the causal relationships between changes in the climate and their influence on the course of human events leading to war.

Even though the vast majority of scientists agree that humankind's carbon emissions are changing the planet's climate, there will always be sufficient numbers of qualified dissenters to provide ammunition for those whose livelihoods, investments or ideologies depend on the economic status quo. Often, those with the greatest interest in maintaining this status quo are those who have derived the most wealth from it – providing them the financial firepower to amplify their minority views. 'It is difficult to get a man to understand something, when his salary depends on his not understanding it,' said the socialist author Upton Sinclair. Sadly, this remains true.

Were the problem confined to those who deny the existence of climate change outright, it might be surmountable. More dangerous are the greater numbers of people who are persuaded by the reality of anthropomorphic climate change, but who are also convinced that multilateral treaties such as the Kyoto Protocol and the Paris Climate Agreement are sufficient to turn the tide. Many believe that such accords, coupled with technological fixes such as the expansion of renewable energy from sources such as solar and wind power, will solve the problem.

This is unlikely to be true, unless world politics undergoes a very rapid evolution. Latterly, the debate over climate change has become so polarized along partisan lines that some major countries are tearing up their participation in such accords as a result of little more than a change in government. Critics were vocal in 2017 when US President Donald Trump cancelled his country's participation in the Paris Climate Agreement, but his move was not unprecedented. Six years earlier, Canada had withdrawn from the Kyoto pact.

The more that progressives, liberals and leftists attack conservatives for not caring enough about the environment, the more conservatives come to suspect their opponents of using climate change as a ruse to promote a political agenda of higher taxes, larger government and invasive regulation. Concerted action against climate change has fallen victim to the minefield that is the US culture wars, a term that describes the hyper-polarized, deeply personalized and gratuitously antagonistic state of current American politics.

Before his election as president in 2016, Trump devoted much time to accusing his Democrat predecessor Barack Obama of being a 'secret Muslim'. It should perhaps have been little surprise, then, that when Trump became president, many Democrats retaliated by accusing him of being a Russian secret agent, on the basis of meetings between his campaign team and Russian officials. In this context, claim and counterclaim begin to lose all sense of reality. The reality of the threat to our environment has become a 'post-truth' debating point.

Back to the future

If humankind is to confront the threat of our planet's destruction as a viable habitat for human life, this era of radical polarization must come to an end. Peace activists have a role and a responsibility in ending the cycle of demonization, hyper-partisanship and hyperbole that has turned US politics into a circus in which one side's core values are denigrated by the other side simply for the sake of it, irrespective of facts and reason. This observation applies to all sides of the political spectrum.

A different world is possible. Not so long ago strong leaders could work across not only party lines but huge ideological gulfs. The 1987 Montreal Protocol demonstrated how governments of radically differing complexions could work together.

In 1974, the Mexican chemist Mario J Molina and his US research partner F Sherwood Rowland published research showing that chlorofluorocarbon gases, known as CFCs, were creating a giant abscess in the earth's ozone layer, a layer of the stratosphere that shields life on earth from the intensity of the sun's ultraviolet radiation.

At once, their findings attracted extensive and hostile lobbying by producers of aerosol sprays and refrigerators, which used the CFC chemicals extensively in their products. Molina and Rowland were criticized by industry-affiliated scientists. Their attempts to warn the world of the danger drew allegations that they were hungry for publicity. CFC-producing industries formed a lobbying group to petition against action against the chemicals. With the Cold War still ongoing, the head of one aerosol company alleged that their research was 'orchestrated by the Ministry of Disinformation of the KGB'.[7]

Yet the scientists had a powerful friend. Better known for tax cuts and deregulation, the Republican President Ronald Reagan resisted industry pressure and championed the need for a ban on CFCs, along with his appointee as head of the US Environmental Protection Agency, Lee Thomas, and his Secretary of State, George Shultz. The US, like most countries, had already banned CFCs from aerosol cans in 1978, under the Carter administration, but a blanket ban was a much bigger step.

The debate shifted dramatically in 1985, when three scientists at the British Antarctic Survey published research that showed a giant hole in the ozone layer emerging over the South Pole. Their findings shocked the world. Suddenly, there was impetus for a global agreement, but the scale of the Montreal Protocol's achievement should not be underestimated, given the context of communist and capitalist superpowers. Molina and Rowland would later win the Nobel Prize for Chemistry for their crucial intervention.

The Montreal Protocol is often hailed as the most successful international accord in human history. Not only did it reverse the expansion of the ozone hole over Antarctica, but recent studies suggest it also slowed the rate of global warming in the 1990s, possibly by a greater degree than the 1992 Kyoto Protocol that addressed humanmade climate change specifically.[8]

Its political lessons are almost as important as its practical effects. The Montreal Protocol showed that even rightwing governments such as those of Ronald Reagan and Britain's Margaret Thatcher could be persuaded to act decisively in an environmental emergency, if the urgency and the causal relationships were made sufficiently clear. It demonstrated that Western conservatives could even persuade hostile countries, such as the Soviet Union, that had radically different political economies, to join their cause. How can peace activists shape the political environment to restore such enlightened problem-solving?

The role of peace

In a sane world, an American who worried about the threat posed by North Korea's nuclear weapons would worry just as much about the outbreak of wars due to parts of the planet becoming uninhabitable. This is why peace activists are so critical to the debate: we are uniquely positioned to explain to security-minded conservatives why they should worry about environmental change.

Britain's domestic intelligence agency has a maxim: 'Society is only ever four meals away from anarchy'. Even the most outwardly stable and prosperous society is liable to collapse when parents find they are unable to feed their children, and the state cannot immediately redress the situation. It is a maxim worth pondering, particularly so in relation to the vast stocks of coal, oil and gas that humanity burns its way through each year.

The worst droughts ever to hit the US came in the 1930s. A so-called 'Dust Bowl' developed in western states, blowing away topsoil, driving farmers off their land and forcing many to travel across the country for new sources of income. The suspicion, violence and hardship experienced by these farmers was immortalized by John Steinbeck in his novel *The Grapes of Wrath*. At the time, the book was criticized by many in the US for supposedly stirring communist sympathies.

The worst drought of the Dust Bowl years came in 1934. It is a record that is likely to be broken soon. According to Nasa, 17 of the 18 warmest years in the 136-year record have occurred since 2001.[9] Nasa's findings are broadly consistent with oceanographic data compiled by the US National Oceanic and Atmospheric Administration, as well as with data collected by other countries and institutions.

A preview of the type of violence produced by climate change arrived in 2016 in the Indian city of Bengaluru, formerly known as Bangalore. The southern city is a poster-child for India's technology revolution – a rapidly growing hub of information technology outsourcing and rising prosperity. Yet in the countryside of the surrounding state of Karnataka, a different story was unfolding.

Farmers were reeling from a second successive failure of the monsoon rains. Crops were dying. The ground was parched, and paddy fields were dry. The final straw came in September 2016, when India's Supreme Court ordered the state to release water from its reservoirs to the neighbouring state of Tamil Nadu, where farmers were also suffering severe shortages of irrigation water.

Hours after the court's decision, Bengaluru erupted into rioting. Protesters set cars and buses alight, blockading roads with burning tyres, attacking Tamil-owned premises and vehicles and fighting with police. One protester died in the violence, which prompted police to impose an emergency law on the city to enhance their own powers.

There was no question that the violence stemmed from water scarcity. Yet those who wished to deny the second inference – that the water scarcity was a result of global warming – would still have plenty of other explanations they could fall back on. They could blame 'over-population', the historically variable nature of the monsoon rains, the country's outmoded irrigation systems, or the corruption that plagues the administration thereof. They could also blame India's low levels of education, which allow populist demagogues to compress complex debates into simple good-versus-evil stories that catalyse violence.

There would be some truth to all these observations, assisting those who wish to deny the earth's rising temperatures any role in the fatal unrest. Climate activists sometimes fall into the opposite trap. They place too much emphasis on the single factor that aids their agenda, while downplaying the others. Peace activists must not make this error. Instead we must candidly admit that the causes of violence are often complex and manifold, while emphasizing a prudential duty of care for the environment that if neglected risks being the straw that breaks the back of a great many camels. In the words of the US military, climate change is a threat-multiplier.[10]

In 2015 researchers from Columbia University published research in the *Proceedings of the National Academy of Sciences* that suggested that a drought that lasted between 2006-09 in Syria was caused by global warming, and that it contributed to the 2011 outbreak of civil war by forcing millions of farmers off their land and into the cities, as per *The Grapes of Wrath*.[11]

Inevitably, other researchers challenged this causal chain. The climatologist Mike Hulme and the international relations professor Jan Selby joined forces to point out that there was not much evidence for displaced farmers igniting the conflict.[12] They also questioned the numbers of farmers giving up their land, and their motives for doing so, arguing that urbanization had predated the drought and was more a function of economic liberalization.

How should peace campaigners respond to such causal controversies? The answer must be to view the prevention of climate change as precautionary, much as eliminating nuclear weapons is precautionary. Logical principles are key. If sufficient mountains of coal and lakes of oil are burnt, over a long enough period, the climate is very likely to change, just as, if enough countries possess nuclear weapons, over a long-enough time horizon, they will eventually be used. Offering highly specific climatic or geopolitical scenarios in the short-term can be counterproductive when it comes to mass persuasion, insofar as they can be challenged by alternative narratives and can draw accusations of opportunism.

A second imperative is to persuade conservatives that the risks of climate change contribute to armed conflict. In this regard, citing the views of senior military personnel is likely to prove effective. The Pentagon has repeatedly warned over many years that climate change raises the risks of natural disasters, in particular flooding from rising sea levels, which have the potential to cause the mass dislocation of human populations in a way that will lead to armed conflict.[13, 14] As noted in the first chapter, by understanding the military's psychological appeal, peace activists can use this to strengthen their arguments, and climate change is a good example of this.

'Climate change is impacting stability in areas of the world where our troops are operating today,' said James Mattis, the US Secretary for Defense and a retired marine general, in congressional testimony in March 2017. It is notable that the man who appointed Mattis does not agree with him. President Trump has described climate change as 'a hoax' invented by China to render US manufacturing uncompetitive. Global climate-change accords such as Kyoto and Paris set lower emissions standards for developing countries such as China than for advanced economies such as the US, feeding the anger of the struggling American workers who elected Trump.

Such treaties have other deficiencies. Writing in the *New Internationalist*, Nick Buxton recorded in 2015 how the climate change accords exempt the world's militaries from reducing their emissions.[15] He noted that the US military, the world's largest single consumer of fossil fuels, used some 117 million barrels of oil in 2011, only slightly less than all the cars in Britain combined.

The US military is attempting to reduce its consumption, both to cut costs and to reduce emissions – its energy usage has been falling since 1975.[16] The same, however, may not be true of military complexes elsewhere in the world, where governments cannot afford to replace ageing, fuel-intensive equipment with cleaner models but which nevertheless are reluctant to disarm when faced with America's ever-rising military expenditure and might. In the case of China and India, the rapid expansion of their military strength comes with an attendant increase in their consumption of fossil fuels.

Wars themselves tend to cause massive releases of greenhouse gases, perhaps best visualized by the burning oil wells of the first Gulf War. Oil is also a key driver of conflict and political repression, as groups fight over what remains the most vital input in the world economy, and in the case of some countries their only fountain of wealth.

Peace, therefore, can be promoted by democratizing and diversifying energy sources via the conversion of military industries into those building renewable sources of power, such as wind turbines, solar panels, hydropower and other new technologies, that can liberate the world from its avidity for crude oil. Investments in these technologies can be viewed as pro-peace as well as ecologically wise. No-one wants a future where people kill each other over water, where inhabited islands disappear beneath the waves, where chaotic mass migrations see millions fleeing 'dust bowl' countries confronted by armed soldiers threatening them with death by another means. Peace activism and environmental activism are no longer easily separable.

---

1 BP, 'Statistical Review of Oil Production', nin.tl/bp-oil-production
2 International Energy Agency, 'World Total Coal Production – 1971-2016', nin.tl/iea-coal-production **3** BP, 'Natural Gas – BP Statistical Review of World Energy 2018', nin.tl/bp-natural-gas **4** Siegel, Ethan, 2017, 'How Much CO_2 Does A Single Volcano Emit?', *Forbes*, 6 June, nin.tl/volcano-co2
5 Gupta, Amrita, 2016, 'The Third World War Will be About Water', Carnegie Council, nin.tl/water-wars **6** Guarino, Ben, 2018, 'The classic explanation for the Black Death plague is wrong, scientists say', *Washington Post*, 16 January, nin.tl/black-death **7** Jones, Lanie, 1988, 'Ozone Warning: He Sounded Alarm, Paid Heavy Price', *Los Angeles Times*, 14 July, nin.tl/ozone-warning
8 Than, Ker, 2013, 'Montreal Protocol Helped Slow Down Global Warming', *National Geographic*, 11 November, nin.tl/montreal-protocol **9** Nasa, 'Global Temperature', climate.nasa.gov/vital-signs/global-temperature
10 Bryan, Joe, 2017, 'Climate Change as a Threat Multiplier', Atlantic Council, 16 November, nin.tl/climate-change-threat **11** Kelley, Colin P et al, 2015, 'Climate change in the Fertile Crescent and implications of the recent Syrian drought', PNAS, 23 February, nin.tl/fertile-crescent **12** Selby, Jan and Hulme, Mike, 2015, 'Is climate change really to blame for Syria's civil war?', *The Guardian*, 29 November, nin.tl/syria-climate-change **13** Reuters, 2018, 'Climate change threatens half of US bases worldwide, Pentagon report finds', *The Guardian*, 31 January, nin.tl/us-bases **14** United Nations, 2014,

'Climate Change Threatens National Security Says Pentagon', 14 October, nin.tl/national-security **15** Buxton, Nick, 2015, 'The elephant in Paris – the military and greenhouse gas emissions', *New Internationalist*, 19 November, nin.tl/paris-elephant **16** US Energy Information Administration, 2015, 'Defense Department energy use falls to lowest level since at least 1975', 5 February, nin.tl/energy-fall

Epilogue
Making it Happen

Much is said about a culture of peace. There is one very specific question that this culture must address. What do we want out of life? Humanity, that is.

The essence of politics is to answer that question on behalf of humanity as a whole. This can seem presumptuous, even arrogant. But it is necessary.

So let us suggest some answers.

People want clean water, clean air, fertile soil and protection from the elements. We want a stable climate, and protection from that small minority of other humans who wish us harm, or who have a psychological illness that renders them a threat to others.

We want to live in democracies that offer equal participation to every adult, regardless of their gender, sexuality, race, creed or ideology. We trust each other to make collective decisions on who leads us, even if we sometimes disagree with the outcome. We do not desire a political system that promotes only the most thick-skinned, unscrupulous, Machiavellian and wealthiest characters, who will then collude as a class to monopolize power.

We want work, but work that bears some clear connection to improving our own lives and those of the people around us. We want our neighbours to have the same opportunities, so that those with a talent for chemistry, or philosophy, or equity analysis, or playing the banjo, can pursue their talents without fear of destitution or political repression.

We also want plentiful spare time, to spend with friends and relatives, to care for the old and infirm, and to enjoy cultural pursuits. We desire foreign travel, yet we also treasure our own local customs, faiths and rituals, because it is important to have a sense of a home.

We desire a healthcare system that caters to both poor and rich, an education system that cultivates the talents of all students, rather than confusing wealth with intelligence, and a culture that respects learning but acknowledges that formal qualifications are not the only measure of success or intellect, and that artistry, perseverance, optimism and empathy are every bit as vital. While we understand that it is difficult to achieve absolute parity of wealth, money should not define access to opportunity.

We want safety and security for our countries, and the world as a whole. Ongoing conflicts and militarization, particularly in the Middle East and Asia, are ripping apart the peaceful fabric of our global society. A high level of violence comes with economic costs, which the Global Peace Index estimates at around $14.76 trillion for 2017.

This vision is not that ambitious. It is by no means impossible to achieve. The world's most successful societies have made great strides towards it, and even many poor countries are not as far away from it as we think.

But nowhere in this vision is there room for war. War is a perverse luxury we cannot afford.

To reinforce this message, let us look in more detail at the findings of the Costs of War project at Brown University. As noted earlier, as of November 2018 it placed the costs to the US taxpayer of the wars since 2001 at almost $6 trillion. Its research found that the figure would expand by a further $700 billion by 2023, and that over the next 35 years, $1 trillion alone would be spent on caring for the injured veterans of the conflicts and their families.[1]

This is actually quite a narrow definition of the price tag, given it omits:

'...*many other expenses, such as the macroeconomic costs to the US economy; the opportunity costs of not investing war dollars in alternative sectors; future interest on war borrowing; and local government and private war costs.*'

The cost of the wars has been funded almost entirely by borrowing. The study predicts that by 2053, the interest payments on the accumulated debt will have reached $7.9 trillion.[2] And who gets those interest payments? By definition, the people from whom the US government borrows are those who have cash to spare – in other words, people who are already financially well off. It is these individuals and corporations who will pocket this $7.9 trillion in interest payments. The debt makes the rich richer. Had the wars been funded by tax increases on the wealthy, the opposite would be true.

Once the debt has been accumulated, its enormous size gives conservatives an excuse to cut social benefits for the poor. 'National debt growing due to Social Security and Medicare,' reported the newspaper *USA Today* in August 2018 in an opinion piece that described cuts to welfare as 'inevitable', and which urged Washington to cut payments to the poor as quickly as possible. Likewise, the US Chamber of Commerce – the country's main business lobby – blames 'entitlement' spending, rather than the country's bloated military and expensive war-mongering, for the gigantic national debt.

High costs in war and war-related spending pose a national security concern because they are unsustainable, says the Watson Institute's report:

'The public will be better served by the increased transparency and by the development of a comprehensive strategy to end the wars and deal with other urgent national security priorities.'[1]

This is not only an American prestige. On the other side of the Atlantic, the idea of a 'European army' is being pushed to restore the fortunes of the EU, which is mired in a number of crises. In late 2018, facing pitifully low domestic popularity ratings, President Emmanuel Macron of France called for the creation of such a military entity to protect Europe against not only Russia, but also Trump's America. Plans for such a military are more advanced than many realize.

In June 2017 the EU announced the launch of a European Defence Fund, which will receive €5.5 billion ($6.25 billion) every year.[3] Polish commissioner Elżbieta Bień kowska described it as:

> 'A game-changer for the EU's strategic autonomy and the competitiveness of Europe's defence industry – including the many SMEs and mid-cap companies forming the European defence supply chain.'

In other words, there was scarcely any pretence that the money was for anything except lining the pockets of Europe's military sector. In August 2018, Germany's finance minister Olaf Scholz called for the 'consolidation' of Europe's defence industry, instead of it being fragmented between individual EU members. Such 'consolidation' would see the creation of EU-wide corporate defence giants to rival the major US conglomerates.

All this has not gone unnoticed by the peace movement. The European Network Against Arms Trade (ENAAT) said the 'corporate capture over EU military-related initiatives is staggering'. It suggested the fund was lobbied into existence by an EU advisory group that included nine industry representatives, six of which are now receiving EU funding from the new defence fund.

It stands to reason that resources devoted to war cannot be used to realize the vision we seek. Military drains the energy of societies. Wars ruin them. There is always a better way. Trillions wasted on military spending can be used to build a sustainable peace economy which will provide a good standard of living for all and works for peace on earth.

Consider for a moment that NATO demands that its members waste two per cent of their economies on military outlay. Two per cent might not sound much. But replicated on a global scale, it amounts to $1.5 trillion each year. That's enough to give every person living in Somalia a lump sum of

$100,000. The next year we could give the same amount to every man, woman and child in Cambodia. The year after that, Haiti and Eritrea combined.

This sketches the colossal waste of productive resources being poured into weapons systems that, by the time they are deployed, will be obsolescent anyway. As we have seen, technology is producing a new breed of cheap, nimble, automated killing machines that render bombers, destroyers, tanks and rockets as relevant to the concept of security as swords, halberds and catapults.

That the NATO two per cent is not seen as a waste by the general public is because economics has been rigged to count unproductive activity as if it were somehow beneficial, and because war has been romanticized in the male psyche. Peace activists must understand the challenge that confronts us: we need to change the system by which our society judges economic and social success. This means waging a whole-of-society campaign to inject sense and decency into an elite class that seems unable to question received wisdom. To cajole, persuade and, if needs must, embarrass the powerful, while sabotaging the false narrative that time and again tempts our leaders to war.

'Where nations work together, hope prevails and collective solutions can be found,' said secretary-general of the UN António Guterres, speaking at the First Paris Forum on Armistice Day, 11 November 2018. He further said: 'Over the past 100 years, the desire to settle conflicts peacefully on the basis of common rules has been converted into a universal system of institutions in the political, economic, social and environmental spheres.'[4]

He emphasized the importance of multilateralism, and how it is indispensable in solving an unprecedented range of problems in international relations, and warned, 'a weakening of the domestic spirit of the compromise and an indifference to collective rules are twin poisons for multilateralism. We need an inclusive multilateralism that is closely related

to civil society and the business community. The legacy
of multilateralism has been invaluable and is at risk of
disintegrating just when it is most needed.'[4]

Our task is to establish a society based on the needs of the
entire planet and beings that inhabit it, a society that is just
and sustainable and one that is not characterized by major
outbreaks of violence and wars.

This is what we mean by cultural change.

If it seems daunting, rest assured, we have allies on our side.
The wealthy and powerful are no monolith. Many of them
are eager to use their wealth to make the world a better place,
as demonstrated by the foundations established by Bill and
Melinda Gates and Hong Kong's Li Ka-shing. Given their vast
tax bills, they have as much interest as anyone in reducing the
influence that military industries exert over our democracies.

Optimism is essential for our new breed of peace-
entrepreneurs. So is perseverance. Building a business takes
time, but they will find friends, supporters and well-wishers,
and people who know someone who can help. Ultimately, our
task is to connect people, so they can bring their different
talents to the same goal.

What would greatly strengthen their hand is a dedicated
Department for Peace. The case for the establishment of a
governmental peace institution is overwhelming. The private
sector and public sector form a mutually virtuous circle, and it
is very difficult for one to exist without the other; establishing
such a circle in the cause of peace is crucial. It would
legitimize, strengthen and embolden us to draw together the
human, financial and creative resources we need to forestall
conflict at home and abroad.

This is only one aspect of the department's work. The
state has a role to play in dealing with the security fears of its
citizens and interrupting violence before it occurs. The notion
of 'safe spaces' has been roundly mocked in recent years, with
rightwing reactionaries dismissing such spaces as havens for
'snowflake' millennials unable to cope with uncomfortable

truths. But the really uncomfortable truth is this – that without safe spaces, either those provided by their parents or by the state, young people become the foot soldiers of crime, urban violence, terrorism and civil war. Whether on the streets of London or Mogadishu, our new Departments for Peace must seek to expand safe spaces. Peace Centres, properly resourced and defended against infiltration by unscrupulous elements, offer a means of allowing poorer youths the same 'safe space' advantages furnished by the parents of their wealthier peers.

Departments for Peace will create positive peace: the attitudes, the institutions and structures that create and sustain peaceful societies. It turns out that, much like the trend of the rich getting richer and the poor getting poorer, the most peaceful countries are getting more peaceful whereas the least peaceful are further declining on the scale.

The least peaceful countries need to be educated and trained on the practicality of nations resolving conflicts without resorting to violence and wars. In other words, the capacity of human society needs to transcend collective violence to become peaceful. They need to value peace; peace is putting the intrinsic sanctity of life, an essential benchmark of human civilization, above the instrumentalism of barbarism and killing.

What we require is an ideological shift of ideas and actions which are necessary to set our minds free to reach the critical mass – allowing us to establish Departments for Peace and Peace Centres, which will become catalysts for our humanity progress towards a less-violent future. We as individuals and civil society have to take steps in the progression from individualism, tribalism and nationalism to globalism, a transition that is essential for giving peace a realistic chance.

Peace can be institutionalized. It can be made to self-sustain just as the military-industrial complex self-sustains. The valour of the battlefield can be transferred to the valour of disaster relief, rescue operations, space exploration and intervention in urban violence. Humanity need not fear a world without war. It is the only future we truly have.

While giving the finishing touches to this book, good and exciting news has come from Ethiopia, where the new history in Africa is being written. Its Prime Minister and inspirational leader Abiy Ahmed is taking revolutionary steps and has created a Ministry for Peace with a senior Cabinet Minister as its head. In his new cabinet reshuffle, he has appointed more women ministers than men and has also appointed Sahie-Work Zewde as the first female President of Ethiopia. In another ground-breaking move, he has brokered peace on a 20-year-old border conflict with neighbouring Eritrea, which claimed more than 100,000 lives. Relations between the two countries have now normalized, with flights and communications resumed, separated families reunited and embassies opened.

It will be fitting to finish the book with a powerful sentiment written by Mary Liebman, a passionate American peace campaigner from Illinois, advocating for the establishment for a Department of Peace in the US:

> '*War is not a natural disaster. It is a manmade disaster, directed and carried out by ordinary people, who are hired and paid by other ordinary people, to make war. It will stop when ordinary people decide that, whatever satisfactions and rewards war may have offered in the past, the risk is now too high and return too low. If you are ready to invest in a new and exciting American Enterprise, you can start by spending an hour telling your congressman why you want a Department of Peace.*'

---

1 Watson Institute, 'Costs of War: Economic Costs', 2016, Brown University, watson.brown.edu/costsofwar/costs/economic **2** US Chamber of Commerce, 'Debt and Deficit', uschamber.com/debt-and-deficit **3** European Commission, 'A European Defence Fund: €5.5 billion per year to boost Europe's defence capabilities', 2017, nin.tl/eu-defence-fund **4** United Nations, 'When nations work together, hope prevails and collective solutions can be found – UN chief tells Peace Forum, marking World War centenary in Paris', 11 November 2018, news.un.org/en/story/2018/11/1025461

Appendices

- Ministry for National Unity, Reconciliation and Peace (MNURP), Solomon Islands, 2002

- Ministry of Peace and Reconstruction, Nepal, 2007

- Ministry of Peace and Justice, Costa Rica, 2009

- Ministry of Peace and CPA (Comprehensive Peace Agreement), South Sudan, 2011

- Ethiopia creates 'Peace Ministry', 2018

- Ministry of Peace Bill, UK, 14 October 2003 – introduced by John McDonnell MP in UK Parliament

- US Department of Peace Bill – History, Support, Provisions of the Kucinich Bill, Previous Proposals

- Ministry for Peace Initiative, Italy

- The Canadian Peace Initiative for Establishment of a Department of Peace within the Government of Canada, 2011

- Global Alliance for Ministries and Infrastructures for Peace (GAMIP)

- The Minister for Peace and Disarmament: An Assessment (Executive Summary) – Conscience UK (2018)

- United Nations General Assembly Draft Resolution (rev. 4/26/10): Building 'Ministries or Departments of Peace' within Governments to Strengthen the Culture of Peace

Ministry for National Unity, Reconciliation and Peace (MNURP), Solomon Islands, 2002

After the conclusion of the Townsville Peace Agreement (TPA) in 2000, a Peace Monitoring Council was established to assist in the implementation of this agreement. In 2002, this was changed into the National Peace Council. The NPC deployed a number of local peace monitors that assisted in local conflict resolution processes. A Ministry for National Unity, Reconciliation and Peace (MNURP) was also established after the TPA, tasked mainly with a reparations program.

However, the TPA was not followed by the necessary assistance in disarmament. This meant that government institutions, which had never been fully developed after independence, were further compromised by corruption and extortion by armed criminals. The compensation payment scheme envisaged in the TPA became severely corrupted and the MNURP lost all credibility.

It was only in 2003 that Australia led the Regional Assistance Mission to Solomon Islands (RAMSI) into the country, effecting a rapid disarmament process, assisted by the NPC. The MNURP regained some of its credibility and began to reassert its role in the peace process. A lack of cooperation between the NPC and the MNURP was at least partially behind the discontinuation of the NPC's mandate in 2007. Although the MNURP established a successor organization in the Peace and Integrity Council, at the time all attention had turned to the process to establish a Truth and Reconciliation Commission, and the PIC remains largely moribund to this day. The TRC was established in 2009 but its work has been delayed and some lack of clarity surrounding its mandate remains. The MNURP has also engaged in national-level reconciliation processes on Malaita and Guadalcanal, and between the two provinces.

Meanwhile, grassroots efforts in reconciliation and

peace-building have continued by civil society and church organizations since the beginning of the conflict in 1999. AusAID also ran a large-scale Community Peace and Restoration Fund between 2000 and 2006 which attempted to strengthen peace-building at the local level through small-scale development projects. Although for many years, state-led and grassroots efforts were proceeding largely parallel to one another, more recently there are signs of more cooperation between grassroots civil society-led peace-building and the MNURP's national level reconciliation programs on Malaita and Guadalcanal.

The 2005 national elections had seen the burning down of half of the capital city of Honiara, especially during the tense period of jockeying for the position of prime minister that followed the polls. In 2010, no violence occurred during or after the national elections – UNDP had supported a nationally-led truth and reconciliation process that helped heal wounds from previous rounds of violence and therefore helped reduce tensions. During and after the elections, a small joint UNDP/ DPA monitoring team assisted national negotiations with observation and facilitation.

In conclusion, there are elements of a peace infrastructure in the Solomon Islands that are beginning to link together. Given the small scale of the country and the serious weaknesses in extending government authority beyond the few main towns, most of this infrastructure consists of civil society and community networks, led in particular through the churches which play a crucial role in community life in the Solomon Islands. Most of this 'infrastructure' remains informal.

Ministry of Peace and Reconstruction, Nepal, 2007

A copy of a letter by Manish Thapa, Coordinator of Nepal Peace Initiative Alliance:

Dear Friends & Colleagues

Namaste

I like to share you exciting news from Nepal and especially one of my initiatives that I launched in Nepal.

As most of you know that, I was lobbying for a state-level Ministry/Department of Peace in Nepal since 2005. I formed a coalition known as "Nepal Peace Initiative Alliance" of 13 organizations which turned my initiative as a truly civil society movement as this coalition consists of NGOs, Academic Institutions, Media Organizations, Faith Based Organizations and Students Organizations including almost all sectors in Nepal. One of our basic objective was lobbying with the Government as well as with Maoist insurgents at that time to start a dialogue for resolution of the conflict in Nepal and creation of state-level Department of Peace (we thought at that point that creation of [a] whole Ministry would be impossible so we demanded at least a Department within a Ministry of Law, Justice & Parliamentary Affairs).

Our initiative was further fuelled when we were invited to join for creation of Global Alliance for Ministries & Departments of Peace (www.mfp-dop.org) which aimed in providing support as well as exchange of ideas and experience for lobbying for such departments & ministries worldwide.

When we achieved our first objectives – dialogue between the Maoists and the 7 key political parties, we were actively supported by the April Revolution which was instrumental in restoring democracy in Nepal.

Then afterwards we were in constant dialogue with 7 key

*Political Parties and Maoists for supporting the creation of
Department of Peace. We had meeting with [the] chief advisor of
the Prime Minister, leading political leaders, civil society leaders
and INGOs. We also had a very fruitful and positive dialogue
with Maoist leaders and their student bodies and we stressed the
need for such [a] Department in Nepal, especially when Nepal
is in transition phase to restore peace, democracy and [the] rule
of law. Similarly we also stressed the instrumental role such [a]
department can play for [a] reconstruction and reconciliation
process, without which the entire peace process will be of no use.*

*We were assured by both sides that they liked the idea and they
were thinking of it. To our surprise, on 31 March 2007, [a] meeting
of key political leaders decided to create a Ministry of Peace &
Reconstruction. We thank all the political leaders and political
parties for this step.*

*Now we can proudly say that we are among the first countries,
along with [the] Solomon Islands to have such [a] Ministry in place
in governmental structures. There are more than 20 countries
including USA, UK, Canada, Uganda, Costa Rica, Australia etc
where there are active campaigns for lobbying for state-level
Ministry/Department of Peace.*

*We would like to thank all our supporters, well-wishers and
especially Global Alliance for this success. Now we are redefining
our strategies for [a] better & prosperous Nepal.*

Thanking you all
Manish Thapa

This letter is reproduced with the permission to reprint from
Prof. Manish Thapa Institute of International Relations, Faculty
of Political Science and International Studies, The University of
Warsaw, Poland.

Ministry of Peace and Justice, Costa Rica, 2009

Costa Rica Creates Department of Peace

On Monday, 14 September [2009], the Costa Rican legislature passed a law changing the name of the country's justice ministry to the Ministry of Justice and Peace, making the Department the first of its kind in Latin America and only the third in the world.

Costa Rica's justice ministry was created to oversee the country's penitentiary systems and supervise research on criminal behaviour, but had no responsibility for crime prevention. A 1998 executive decree addressed this lapse by creating the National Directorate for the Prevention of Crime. The recent legislation takes crime prevention in a new direction, replacing the old directorate with the newly formed Directorate for the Promotion of Peace and the Peaceful Coexistence of Citizens.

'While we talk about prevention of violence, we are experiencing its effects every day. Changing the language and speaking about "promotion of peace" lead[s] us to the roots of the problem,' states the legislation.

The Ministry will take on new responsibilities, including peace promotion, violence prevention (for example, by targeting a recent increase of juvenile offenders), and an emphasis on conflict resolution.

Days after the official creation of its Ministry of Justice and Peace, Costa Rica hosted an international summit for others working to create similar ministries. The Dalai Lama wrote a letter endorsing the summit:

'Peace is not something which exists independently of us, any more than war does. Those who are responsible for creating and keeping the peace are members of our own human family, the society that we as individuals participate in and help to create. Peace in the world thus depends on there being peace in the hearts of individuals. Peace based merely on political considerations or prompted by other compulsions will only be temporary and superficial.'

'With this change in name, the focus on prevention of violence has been shifted to promotion of peace,' says Kelly Isola of the Rasur Foundation, the Costa Rican NGO that proposed the law in 2005. Having a Department of Peace, she said, will enable Costa Rica 'to benefit from international experiences, which demonstrate that a culture of peace has positive effects in the reduction of violence and crime'.

Although campaigns for peace-oriented government departments are under way in 32 countries, including the US, only Nepal and the Solomon Islands have similar ministries.

'This Ministry was not born out of war and conflict, but rather through the commitment to a culture of peace,' Isola says. 'Costa Rica has a long history of being aligned with peace.'

The country's tradition of peace-oriented firsts dates back to 1877, when President Tomás Guardia abolished the death penalty. In 1948, Costa Rica became the first country to formally abolish its armed forces; the Constitution still forbids a standing military. President Oscar Arias won the 1987 Nobel Peace Prize for his leadership on the Esquipulas II Peace Accords, which promoted regional reconciliation, democratization, free elections and arms control in Central America. In 1997, Costa Rica passed a law requiring that peace education be offered in every school and created a place for peaceful conflict resolution in the legal system, which endorses mediation.

In 2004, the National Directorate of Alternative Conflict Resolution was created, and two years later the National Commission for the Prevention of Violence and Promotion of Social Peace was established. The newly overhauled Ministry of Justice and Peace will work with both.

Legislation for the new law was passed just in time for the fourth annual Global Alliance Summit for Ministries and Departments of Peace, held in Costa Rica 17-21 September.

The Global Alliance comprises organizations, citizens and government officials from 35 countries, who work together to establish governmental structures that support a culture of peace.

Written by Susie Shutts. At the time of writing this article, Susie was a web editorial intern at *Yes! Magazine*. This article was originally published by Yes! Media (22 September 2009), copyright ©2018 Yes! Media.
Original URL: yesmagazine.org/peace-justice/costa-rica-creates-department-of-peace

Ministry of Peace and CPA (Comprehensive Peace Agreement), South Sudan, 2011

The Comprehensive Peace Agreement between the government of the Republic of the Sudan and the Sudan People's Liberation Movement/Sudan People's Liberation Army

Chapeau of the comprehensive peace agreement whereas the Government of the Republic of the Sudan (GOS) and the Sudan People's Liberation Movement/Sudan People's Liberation Army (SPLM/A) (hereinafter referred to as the 'Parties'), having met in continuous negotiations between May 2002 and December 2004, in Karen, Machakos, Nairobi, Nakuru, Nanyuki and Naivasha, Kenya, under the auspices of the Inter-Governmental Authority on Development (IGAD) Peace Process, and, in respect of the issues related to the Conflict Areas of Southern Kordofan and Blue Nile States and Abyei Area, under the auspices of the Government of the Republic of Kenya;

Conscious that the conflict in the Sudan is the longest running conflict in Africa; that it has caused tragic loss of life, destroyed the infrastructure of the country, eroded its economic resources and caused suffering to the people of the Sudan;

Mindful of the urgent need to bring peace and security to the people of the Sudan who have endured this conflict for far too long;

Aware of the fact that peace, stability and development are aspirations shared by all people of the Sudan;

In pursuance of the commitment of the Parties to a negotiated settlement on the basis of a democratic system of governance which, on the one hand, recognizes the right of the people of Southern Sudan to self-determination and seeks to make unity attractive during the Interim Period, while at the same time is founded on the values of justice, democracy, good governance, respect for fundamental rights and freedoms of the individual, mutual understanding and tolerance of diversity within the realities of the Sudan;

Recording and reconfirming that in pursuance of this commitment the Parties duly reached agreement on the following texts: the Machakos Protocol, dated 20th July, 2002 which is set out in Chapter I of the Comprehensive Peace Agreement (CPA); the Agreement on Security Arrangements, dated 25th September, 2003 which is set out in Chapter VI of the CPA; the Agreement on Wealth Sharing, dated 7th January, 2004 which is set out in Chapter III of the CPA; the Protocol on Power Sharing, dated 26th May, 2004 which is set out in Chapter II of the CPA; the Protocol on the Resolution of the Conflict In Southern Kordofan and Blue Nile States, dated 26th May, 2004 which is set out in Chapter V of the CPA; and the Protocol on the Resolution of the Conflict in Abyei Area, dated 26th May, 2004 which is set out in Chapter IV of the CPA; and that the Security Council of the United Nations in its Resolution 1574 of 19th November, 2004, took note of these aforementioned Protocols and Agreements;

Recognising that the Parties have concluded an Agreement on a Permanent Ceasefire and Security, Arrangements Implementation Modalities During the Pre-Interim and Interim Periods dated 31st December, 2004 which is set out in Annexure I of the CPA, within the Framework of the Agreement on Security Arrangements of 25th September, 2003;

Further recognising that the Parties have also concluded the Agreement on the Implementation Modalities of the Protocols and Agreements dated 31st December, 2004 which is set out in Annexure Il of the CPA;

Now herein the parties jointly acknowledge that the CPA offers not only hope but also a concrete model for solving problems and other conflicts in the country;

The parties further acknowledge that the successful implementation of the CPA shall provide a model for good governance in the Sudan that will help create a solid basis to preserve peace and make unity attractive and therefore

undertake to fully adhere to the letter and spirit of the CPA
so as to guarantee lasting peace, security for all, justice and
equality in the Sudan;

Now therefore, the parties agree, upon signing this
Agreement, on the following:

(1) The Pre-Interim Period shall commence, and all the
obligations and commitments specified in the CPA shall be
binding in accordance with the provisions thereof;

(2) The CPA shall be comprised of the texts of the Protocols
and Agreements already signed, together with this
Chapeau, the Agreement on Permanent Ceasefire and
Security Arrangements Implementation Modalities and
Appendices as Annexure I and the Agreement on the
Implementation Modalities and the Global Implementation
Matrix and Appendices as Annexure II;

(3) The agreed Arabic and English texts of the CPA shall both
be official and authentic. However, in the event of a dispute
regarding the meaning of any provision of the text, and
only if there is a difference in meaning between the Arabic
and English texts; the English text shall be authoritative as
English was the language of the peace negotiations.

(4) Upon compilation of the official and authentic Arabic and
English texts of the CPA, the initialled copies of both texts
shall be given to both Parties, and copies shall also be
lodged with the United Nations, the African Union, IGAD
Secretariat in Djibouti, the League of Arab States and the
Republic of Kenya.

(5) All persons performing governmental functions shall
continue to do so at the place at which they render
such services or perform such functions unless or until
redeployed or alternative instructions are received in
accordance with the arrangements agreed to by the Parties.

(6) To establish such priority joint task teams, particularly
the Joint National Transitional Team (JNTT), the Abyei
Boundaries Commission (ABC), the Constitutional Task

Team and the Joint Technical Team on 'New National
Currency' as required to facilitate and prepare for the
operationalisation of the Agreement once it is put into force;
(7) To take the necessary steps to ensure the effective
implementation of the Permanent Ceasefire;
(8) To take such steps as are necessary to ensure that
resources and funds are available for the establishment of
the structures, bodies and institutions contemplated by the
CPA especially the establishment of the Government of
Southern Sudan;

The parties express their gratitude for the persistent
efforts of the Facilitators, the IGAD Member States, and the
International Community in assisting the people of the Sudan
to return to peace and stability, and in particular, to the
African Union, IGAD Partners Forum, the United Nations,
and the Governments of Italy, Norway, United Kingdom and
the United States of America for their support for the IGAD
Peace Initiative and their unwavering interest and consistent
endeavours in support of the Peace Process;

The parties jointly appeal to the Regional and International
Community and call on Organizations and States which have
been requested to witness the signing of this Agreement to
provide and affirm their unwavering support to the implementation of the CPA, and further appeal to them to avail resources
for the necessary and urgent programmes and activities of the
transition to peace as contemplated and agreed herein;

The parties recognize the enormity of the tasks that lie
ahead in successfully implementing the Comprehensive Peace
Agreement and in signing below and before the witnesses here
present, they reconfirm their commitment to implement the
Comprehensive Peace Agreement fully and jointly.

H.E. Ali Osman Mohamed Taha
First Vice President of the Republic of the Sudan
On behalf of the Government of the Republic of the Sudan

Dr. John Garang de Mabior
Chairman of the Sudan People's Liberation Movement/Sudan
People's Liberation Army on behalf of the Sudan People's
Liberation Movement/Sudan People's Liberation Army

WITNESSED BY:
H.E. Hon. Mwai Kibaki
President of the Republic of Kenya
On behalf of the IGAD Sub-Committee on the Sudan

H.E. Hon. Yoweri Kaguta Museveni
President of the Republic of Uganda
On Behalf of IGAD Member States

H.E. Mr. Ahmed Aboul Gheit
Egyptian Minister of Foreign Affairs
On behalf of the Government of the Republic of Egypt

Senator Alfredo Mantica
Deputy Minister for Foreign Affairs
On behalf of the Government of Italy

H.E Mr. Fred Racke
Special Envoy of the Netherlands
On behalf of the Royal Kingdom of the Netherlands

H.E. Ms. Hilde F. Johnson
Minister of International Development
On behalf of the Royal Norwegian Government

Right Hon. Hilary Benn, M.P
Secretary of State for International Development
On behalf of the United Kingdom and Northern Ireland

Mr. Colin L. Powell
United States Secretary of State
On behalf of the United States of America

H.E. Mr. Alpha Oumar Konare
Chairperson of the African Union
On behalf of the African Union

Hon. Charles Goerens
Minister of Development Co-operation of Netherlands
On behalf of the European Union

H.E. Ms. Hilde F. Johnson
Minister of International Development
On behalf of the IGAD Partners Forum (IPF)

Senator Alfredo Mantica
Deputy Minister for Foreign Affairs
On behalf of the IGAD Partners Forum (IPF)

H.E Mr. Amre Moussa
Secretary General of the League of Arab States
On behalf of the League of Arab States

H.E. Mr. Jan Pronk
Special Representative of the Secretary General in the Sudan
On behalf of the United Nations

This article was originally published by ReliefWeb (9 January 2005)
and is reproduced with their permission. Original URL: reliefweb.int/
report/sudan/comprehensive-peace-agreement-between-government-
republic-sudan-and-sudan-peoples

Ethiopia creates 'Peace Ministry' to tackle violence in sweeping reshuffle, 2018

Originally published by Reuters, 16 October 2018

Ethiopia's prime minister [Abiy Ahmed] created a new Ministry of Peace and handed half the posts in his cabinet to women in a sweeping cabinet reshuffle on Tuesday as he sought to tackle a wave of ethnic violence.

'The main problem in this country is the lack of peace. This (peace) ministry will be working hard to ensure it prevails,' Abiy told lawmakers.

About 2.2 million people out of a population of 100 million have been displaced by violence since last year, much of it between rival ethnic groups.

The new peace ministry will be led by former parliament speaker Muferiat Kamil, with her office now presiding over Ethiopia's Federal Police Commission, the National Intelligence and Security Service and the Information Network Security Agency, the government said.

Some analysts criticized the new body's composition saying it was dominated by the security services and lacked civilian input. 'It is highly dominated by political appointees. While it can contribute a lot, it could do with the expertise of technocrats in the bid to find peace,' said Yonas Ashine, a politics lecturer at Addis Ababa University.

Since his appointment, Abiy has made peace with neighbor Eritrea and presided over the partial privatization of economic sectors such as telecommunications.

The 42-year-old has also extended an olive branch to several rebel groups, promised to follow a policy of reconciliation and rein in the powerful security agencies. Yet the changes have not stopped ethnically charged violence, some of which escalated since he was named premier.

Former construction minister Aisha Mohammed was named

defense minister - the first woman to hold that position in the country.

Ahmed Shide, who has previously served as a deputy minister of finance and a government spokesman, replaced Abraham Tekeste as finance minister.

The economy has grown by nearly 10 per cent on average for the past decade, official data shows, but the recent unrest has led to concerns over its long-term stability.

Abiy merged ministries to cut the cabinet to 20 from 28 and for the first time handed half of the top jobs to women.

He named new ministers of agriculture, culture and tourism, education, labor, mines, planning and development, revenue, science, trade, transport, urban development, and women's affairs – a mixture of new names and reshuffled ministers.

He kept Workneh Gebeyehu as foreign minister, Amir Aman as health minister and Seleshi Bekele as water and electricity minister, as well as Berhanu Tsegaye as attorney general.

Written by: Aaron Maasho. Edited by: Duncan Miriri, Andrew Heavens and David Stamp
Original URL: reuters.com/article/us-ethiopia-politics/ethiopia-creates-peace-ministry-to-tackle-violence-in-sweeping-reshuffle-idUSKCN1MQ1M6

Ministry of Peace Bill, UK, 14 October 2003 – introduced by John McDonnell MP in UK Parliament

A BILL TO Establish a Ministry of Peace with the function of promoting conflict resolution and the avoidance of military conflict

Be it enacted by the Queen's most Excellent Majesty, by and with the advice and consent of the Lords Spiritual and Temporal, and Commons, in this present Parliament assembled, and by the authority of the same, as follows:—

1 The Ministry of Peace

(1) There shall be a Ministry of Peace which shall have the following functions—
   (a) to advise the Prime Minister and the Secretary of State for Foreign and Commonwealth Affairs during a military conflict or when a military conflict is likely;
   (b) to advise Ministers of the Crown about non-violent conflict resolution in respect of the negotiation of treaties and at other times as may be specified in the Prime Minister's report under subsection 3(1) below;
   (d) to educate the public about conflict resolution;
   (e) to facilitate public participation in the development and implementation of solutions to local, regional, national, and international conflicts; and
   (f) to advise—
      (i)   the Secretary of State for Education and Skills on the preparation of programmes of study relating to peace education to be included in the National Curriculum;
      (ii) the Department of Education in Northern Ireland on the preparation of programmes of study relating to peace education to be included in the National Curriculum; and

(iii) the Scottish Executive Education Department
on the preparations of guidelines relating to peace
education.

(2) The Prime Minister may by order create additional
functions for the Ministry of Peace.

(3) An order made under this section shall not come into
effect unless a draft of it has been laid before, and
approved by resolution of, each House of Parliament.

2 Commission for Peace

As part of the Ministry for Peace there shall be established a
Commission for Peace with the following functions, namely
to—

(a) monitor and report to Parliament from time to time on the
effectiveness of the Government and local government
in preventing and resolving conflict at local, regional,
national and international levels

(b) provide advice to the Secretary of State;

(c) seek to improve the links between universities, the
research councils and other research institutions and
local, national and international organisations concerned
with the promotion of peace or the prevention and
resolution of conflict;

(d) assist non-governmental organisations in analysing,
sharing their experience of, and learning from, peace-
building work in regions where there are conflicts;

(e) determine criteria for the establishment of local and
regional peace commissions, with discretion to provide
financial or other assistance to such commissions where
these criteria are satisfied;

(f) facilitate collaboration between organisations concerned
with the promotion of peace or the prevention and
resolution of conflict and the Government; and

(g) encourage public support for peace-building.

3 Report and draft Bill on the work of the Ministry for Peace and the Commission for Peace

(1) Within 100 days after this Act is passed the Prime Minister shall publish a report ("the Report") and a draft Bill ("the Bill") which shall include—

(a) the further steps which need to be taken to establish a Ministry for Peace and a Commission for Peace within the Ministry for Peace; and

(b) which of the matters listed in Schedule 1 should be addressed by the Ministry for Peace and what additional functions it should have.

(2) When preparing the Report and Bill, the Prime Minister shall have regard to the sources and texts listed in Schedule 2.

(3) Before laying the Report before Parliament and publishing the Bill the Prime Minister shall consult as many persons falling within each of the categories listed in Schedule 3 as is reasonably practicable.

4 Financial provision

There shall be paid out of money provided by Parliament—

(a) any expenditure of the Secretary of State in consequence of this Act; and

(b) any increase attributable to this Act in the sums payable out of money so provided by virtue of any other Act.

5 Citation, extent and commencement

(1) This Act may be cited as the Ministry of Peace Act 2003.

(2) This Act extends to England, Northern Ireland, Scotland and Wales.

(3) This Act shall come into force on the date on which it is passed.

SCHEDULES
SCHEDULE 1

Matters which might be addressed by, and potential functions of, the Ministry of Peace for the purposes of section 3

Within the United Kingdom
1. In relation to the United Kingdom, the following are to be considered as potential matters to be addressed by the Ministry of Peace—
    (a) domestic violence, including spousal abuse, child abuse, and mistreatment of older people;
    (b) drug and alcohol abuse;
    (c) crime, punishment, and rehabilitation;
    (d) the implements of violence, including handguns;
    (e) school violence and gangs;
    (f) violence on the grounds of sex, race, colour, nationality, ethnic or national origin, religion or belief, sexual orientation, disability and police-community relations disputes;
    (g) unlawful violence against animals; and
    (h) the use of excess force by employees or agents of public authorities.

International relations
2. In relation to international relations, the following are to be considered as potential matters to be addressed by the Ministry of Peace—
    (a) potential and existing conflicts that threaten or appear to threaten the United Kingdom whether from sovereign nations or other external influences;
    (b) other existing, potential or threatened international armed conflicts; and
    (c) post-conflict reconstruction and demobilisation in the United Kingdom and other countries.

Public education and participation

3. In relation to public education and participation, the
   following are to be considered as potential matters to be
   addressed by the Ministry of Peace—

   (a) with a view to the inclusion of the subject as a
       foundation subject in the National Curriculum pursuant
       to section 354 of the Education Act 1996 (c. 56) and in
       other levels of education, commissioning research on
       peace education which shall include, but not be limited
       to, studies of—

       (i)   the civil rights movement in the United
       Kingdom and other countries and the contribution
       that individuals and groups have made towards
       advancements in peace;

       (ii) peace agreements and circumstances in which
       peaceful intervention has worked to stop conflict; and

       (iii) practical conflict resolution tools to prevent and
       resolve conflict in domestic, social and commercial
       environments; and

   (b) educating and enabling the general public to participate
       in the development and implementation of solutions
       to local, regional and national issues facing the United
       Kingdom and other countries.

Research and the media

4. In relation to research and the media, the following are to
   be considered as potential matters to be addressed by the
   Ministry of Peace—

   (a) the development and implementation of approaches
       to peaceful co-existence and non-violent conflict
       resolution;

   (b) the role of the media in the resolution of conflict both
       in the United Kingdom and in other countries, with
       special reference to—

       (i)   seeking assistance in the design and
       implementation of non-violent policies from journalist;

      (ii) studying the role of the media in the escalation and de-escalation of conflict within the United Kingdom and in other countries; and

      (iii) making recommendations to professional media organisations in order to provide opportunities to increase media awareness of peace-building initiatives;

(c) the impact of new technologies on the creation and maintenance of peace within the United Kingdom and in other countries, including analysis of technologies in transportation, communications and energy that—

      (i)   are non-violent in their application; and

      (ii) encourage the conservation and sustainability of natural resources in order to prevent future conflicts regarding scarce resources;

(d) the impact of war, especially upon—

      (i)   the physical and mental condition of children;

      (ii) the environment; and

      (iii) public health

(e) effective community peace-building activities;

(f) human rights abuses, both within the United Kingdom and in other countries; and

(g) the scarcity of natural resources as a source of conflict, including but not limited to, studies of—

      (i)   non-violent prevention of such scarcity and peaceful intervention in the case of such scarcity;

      (ii) the development of assistance for people experiencing such scarcity, whether due to armed conflict, inequitable distribution of resources or natural causes; and

      (iii) the sustainability and management of the distribution of overseas development funds from national and international agencies, the conditions regarding the receipt of such funds and the impact of those conditions on the peace and stability of the recipient nations.

Consultation

The following are to be considered as potential matters relating to non-violent conflict resolution about which the Ministry of Peace should be consulted at relevant times by the Prime Minister—

(a) a conflict or an impending conflict between the United Kingdom and any other government or group of individuals; and

(b) drafting bilateral or multilateral peace treaties and agreements.

SCHEDULE 2

Sources and texts for purposes of section 3

1. The Seville Statement on Violence, Spain, 1986 (subsequently adopted by UNESCO at the Twenty-Fifth Session of the General Conference on 16 November 1989.

2. The Hague Agenda for Peace and Justice for the 21st Century (UN Ref A/54/98) and Supplement).

3. Children and Violence – Report of the Commission on Children and Violence convened by the Gulbenkian Foundation, 1995.

4. Declaration and Agenda for Action of the UN Millennium Forum on the Strengthening of the UN for the 21st Century, 2000.

5. European Convention for the Protection of Human Rights and Fundamental Freedoms, 1950.

6. European Council Resolution on Integrating Gender in Development, 1995.

7. European Parliament Resolution on Gender Aspects on Conflict Resolution and Peace Building.

8. European Parliament Resolution on the Application of the Geneva Convention relating to the Status of Refugees, 1984.

9. European Parliament Resolution on Women in Decision-making, 2000.

10. European Parliament Resolutions (2) on the Rape of Women in the Former Yugoslavia, 1992; 1993.
11. Geneva Conventions and additional Protocols, 1949; 1977.
12. International Convention on the Elimination of All Forms of Discrimination Against Women, 1979.
13. International Convention on the Elimination of All Forms of Race Discrimination, 1965.
14. International Covenant on Civil and Political Rights, 1966.
15. International Covenant on Economic, Social, and Cultural Rights, 1966.
16. Outcome documents of public hearings on gender specific human rights violations and rape as a war crime in Bosnia, 1993; 1995.
17. Rome Statute of the International Criminal Court, 1998.
18. The Beijing Declaration and Platform for Action, 1995.
19. The proposed UN Commission on Peace and Crisis Prevention.
20. The Rio Declaration, 1992.
21. UN Convention on the Rights of the Child, 1989.
22. UN General Assembly Convention Against Torture and Other Cruel, Inhumane or Degrading Treatment or Punishment, 1984.
23. UN General Assembly Declaration 3318 on the Protection of Women and Children in Emergency and Armed Conflict, 1974.
24. UN General Assembly Resolution 3519 on Women's Participation in the Strengthening of International Peace and Security, 1975.
25. UN Security Council Resolution 1265 on the Protection of Civilians in Armed Conflict, 1999.
26. United Nations Security Council Resolution 1325 – Women Peace and Security.
27. Universal Declaration of Human Rights, 1948.
28. Vienna Declaration and Program of Action, 1993.

SCHEDULE 3
Categories of persons to be consulted for
the purposes of section 3

1. Public authorities including Ministers of the Crown and Government Departments, Ministers of the Northern Ireland Assembly, the Scottish Administration, the National Assembly for Wales.
2. Local authorities.
3. Voluntary bodies.
4. Bodies representing the interests of persons carrying out business in the UK.
5. Governing bodies of schools and institutions of further and higher education.
6. Political parties.
7. Women's organisations.
8. Bodies representing the interests of different religious groups.

US Department of Peace Bill – History, Support, Provisions of the Kucinich Bill, Previous Proposals

History

The peace movement in the United States has a proposed legislative history that dates to the first years of the republic:

- 1793: Dr Benjamin Rush, Founding Father (signer of the Declaration of Independence), wrote an essay titled 'A plan of a Peace-Office for the United States'. Dr Rush called for equal footing with the Department of War and pointed out the effect of doing so for the welfare of the United States in promoting and preserving perpetual peace in the United States. First published in a 1793 almanac that Benjamin Banneker authored, the plan stated:

  1. Let a Secretary of Peace be appointed to preside in this office; ...let him be a genuine republican and a sincere Christian...

  2. Let a power be given to the Secretary to establish and maintain free schools in every city, village and township in the United States; ...Let the youth of our country be instructed in reading, writing, and arithmetic, and in the doctrines of a religion of some kind; the Christian religion should be preferred to all others; for it belongs to this religion exclusively to teach us not only to cultivate peace with all men, but to forgive – nay more, to love our very enemies...

  3. Let every family be furnished at public expense, by the Secretary of this office, with an American edition of the Bible...

  4. Let the following sentence be inscribed in letters of gold over the door of every home in the United States: The Son of Man Came into the World, Not To Destroy Men's Lives, But To Save Them.

  5. To inspire a veneration for human life, and a horror at the shedding of human blood, let all those laws be repealed which authorize juries, judges, sheriffs, or hangmen to

assume the resentments of individuals, and to commit murder in cold blood in any case whatever...

6. To subdue that passion for war... militia laws should everywhere be repealed, and military dresses and military titles should be laid aside...

- 1925: Carrie Chapman Catt, founder of the League of Women Voters, at the Cause and Cure for War Conference, publicly suggested a cabinet-level Department of Peace and secretary of peace be established.
- 1926/1927: Kirby Page, author of *A National Peace Department*, wrote, published and distributed a proposal for a cabinet-level Department of Peace and secretary of peace.
- 1935: Senator Matthew M. Neely (D-West Virginia) wrote and introduced the first bill calling for the creation of a United States Department of Peace. Reintroduced in 1937 and 1939.
- 1943: Senator Alexander Wiley (R-Wisconsin) spoke on the Senate floor calling for the United States of America to become the first government in the world to have a secretary of peace.
- 1945: Representative Louis Ludlow (D-Indiana) re-introduced a bill, S. 1237, to create a United States Department of Peace.
- 1946: Senator Jennings Randolph (D-West Virginia) re-introduced a bill to create a United States Department of Peace.
- 1947: Representative Everett Dirksen (R-Illinois) introduced a bill for 'A Peace Division in the State Department'.
- 1955 to 1968: Eighty-five Senate and House of Representative bills were introduced calling for a United States Department of Peace.
- 1969: Senator Vance Hartke (D-Indiana) and Representative Seymour Halpern (R-New York) re-introduced bills to create a US Department of Peace in the House of Representatives and the Senate. The 14 Senate cosponsors of S. 953, the 'Peace Act', included Birch Bayh (D-IN), Robert

Byrd (D-WV), Alan Cranston (D-CA), Daniel Inouye (D-HI)
and Edmund Muskie (D-ME). The 67 House cosponsors
included Ed Koch of New York, Donald Fraser of Minnesota
and Abner Mikva of Illinois, as well as Republican Pete
McCloskey of California.

- 1979: Senator Spark Matsunaga (D-Hawaii) re-introduced a
  bill, S. 2103, 'Department of Peace Organization Act of 1979'
  to create a US Department of Peace.
- 2001: Representative Dennis Kucinich (D-Ohio)
  re-introduced a bill to create a US Department of Peace.
  This bill has since been introduced in each session of
  Congress from 2001 to 2009. It was re-introduced as HR
  808 on February 3, 2009 and is currently supported by 72
  cosponsors. In July 2008, the first Republican cosponsor,
  Rep Wayne Gilchrest (R-MD) signed on.
- 2005: Senator Mark Dayton (D-Minnesota) introduced
  legislation in the Senate to create a cabinet-level department
  of peace a week after Dennis Kucinich introduced a similar
  bill in the House.

Support

The Peace Alliance and the Student Peace Alliance
organisations support the creation of a US Department
of Peace. Both are national non-profit organizations and
independent grassroots political movements that operate
autonomously. The ongoing movement is supported by several
members of Congress, the late former *CBS Evening News*
anchor Walter Cronkite and author Marianne Williamson.
Also joining the increasing list of national endorsements are
Yoko Ono, Joaquin Phoenix, Frances Fisher and Willie Nelson.
This movement actively lobbies for the endorsements of
congressional leaders and is active in soliciting and receiving
a growing list of bipartisan endorsements from city councils
in California, Florida, Georgia, Illinois, Michigan, New Mexico
and Ohio. Local grassroots chapters have been formed in all
50 states.

Provisions of the Kucinich Bill

Ohio Rep Dennis Kucinich introduced US Department of Peace legislation to Congress in July 2001, two months before the September 11 attacks. Kucinich has reintroduced the legislation every two years since. The bill currently has 52 co-sponsors. Some of the numerous organizations endorsing the legislation include Amnesty International and the National Organization for Women.

This bill includes several additional proposed mandates that would work in partnership with the US Department of State and go beyond the existing mandates of the United States Institute of Peace. Some highlights among the areas of proposed additional responsibility include:

- Provide violence prevention, conflict resolution skills and mediation to America's school children in classrooms as an elective or requirement, providing them with the communication tools they need to express themselves beginning in elementary school through high school.
- Provide support and grants for violence prevention programs addressing domestic violence, gang violence, drug- and alcohol-related violence, and the like.
- To effectively treat and dismantle gang psychology.
- To rehabilitate the prison population.
- To build peace-making efforts among conflicting cultures both here and abroad.
- To support our military with complementary approaches to ending violence.
- Monitoring of all domestic arms production, including non-military arms, conventional military arms, and of weapons of mass destruction.
- Make expert recommendations on the latest techniques for diplomacy, mediation and conflict resolution to the US President for various strategies.
- Assumption of a more proactive level of involvement in the establishment of international dialogues for international conflict resolution (as a cabinet level department).

- Establishment of a US Peace Academy, which among other things would train international peace-keepers.
- Development of an educational media programme to promote nonviolence in the domestic media.
- Monitoring of human rights, both domestically and abroad.
- Making regular recommendations to the President for the maintenance and improvement of these human rights.
- Receiving a timely mandatory advance consultation from the Secretaries of State, and of Defense, prior to any engagement of US troops in any armed conflict with any other nation.
- Establishment of a national Peace Day.
- Participation by the secretary of peace as a member of the National Security Council.
- Expansion of the national Sister City programme.
- Significant expansion of current Institute of Peace programme involvement in educational affairs, in areas such as:
  1. Drug rehabilitation,
  2. Policy reviews concerning crime prevention, punishment, and rehabilitation,
  3. Implementation of violence prevention counselling programmes and peer mediation programmes in schools,
- Also, making recommendations regarding:
  1. Battered women's rights,
  2. Animal rights,
- Various other 'peace related areas of responsibility'.

Proposed funding for a US Department of Peace would initially come from a budget that is defined by the prevention bill as, 'at least 1 per cent of the proposed federal discretionary budget, FY 2008 of which 53 per cent is already allocated to the Department of Defense (budget)'. Whether or not the US Institute of Peace would be promoted to a cabinet-level position, is not addressed by this bill. The Peace Alliance is the National Organization spearheading the passage of the legislation.

Previous proposals

In 1969, Senator Vance Hartke (D-Indiana) introduced the Peace Act (S. 953), to establish a cabinet-level called for the new department to develop 'plans, policies and [programmes] designed to foster peace,' coordinate all US government activities affecting 'the preservation or promotion of peace,' to cooperate with other governments in planning for peaceful conflict resolution, and promote the exchange of ideas between private parties in the US and other countries. The bill further provided for establishment of an International Peace Institute that would train citizens for service, a Peace by Investment Corporation, and the transfer of agencies such as the Peace Corps, Agency for International Development, and the International Agricultural Development Service, to the new Department. The bill received popular support from anti-war groups, Catholic and Baptist publications, author Norman Cousins, and others.

Fiction

The novel *1988* (a fictional work about the upcoming 1988 presidential election published in 1985) by then-Governor of Colorado Richard Lamm, includes a very similar proposal where the third-party presidential candidate in the novel proposes a cabinet-level Agency for US Peace and Conflict Resolution with a secretary of peace who could challenge the secretary of defence when necessary.

Source: Wikipedia en.wikipedia.org/wiki/Department_of_Peace

Ministry for Peace Initiative, Italy

About Ministry for Peace, Italy

To celebrate the 21 September – UN Day of Ceasefire and
Non Violence – we are pleased to inform you of the public
launch of our group working towards creating a Ministry
for Peace in Italy, thus joining the many other groups in
Australia, Canada, Costa Rica, India, Japan, Nepal, Philippines,
Solomon Islands, Uganda, UK [and] US. Ten other countries
are also exploring the idea: Cameroon, Congo, Israel, Liberia,
Netherlands, New Zealand[/Aotearoa], Palestine, Romania,
Spain and Sri Lanka.

In 1999, all the countries at the UN agreed upon the
Declaration and Programme of Action on a Culture of Peace.
This called for everyone – governments, civil society, the
media, parents, teachers, politicians, scientists, artists, NGOs
[and] the UN – to assume responsibility for taking action.
But where are the results?

The goal of a Ministry for Peace is to reduce violence in
all its forms and to convince people that the use of direct
violence as a means to achieve ends is uncivilized and
counter-productive. Our programme is educational and not
party political. It is designed to foster a culture of peace
and to embed non-violent methods and approaches into
all our public institutions, civil society, schools, the arts
and sports.

A Ministry for Peace would be staffed by individuals skilled
in helping others understand the efficacy of non-violent
communication and in resolving conflicts non-violently.
Its work would assist rather than replace that of other
government departments.

We believe that the promotion of a Culture for Peace
needs to start in the schools and, while we acknowledge
that there will always be conflicts in some form or another,
what is important is how we deal with [them]. A Ministry for

Peace Italy would assist the Ministry of Education to create programmes in peace-building skills and how to transform conflicts in a peaceful way.

The initial aims of Ministry for Peace Italy are:

- Strengthen our working group to include those interested.
- Create a Peace Festival dedicated to 'Dialogue'.
- Promote the teaching of peace-building skills in schools and society in general.
- Promote the role of women in conflict prevention and transformation (Article 1325).
- Continue to contribute actively to the Global Alliance and its aims.
- Discuss the possibility of hosting a Summit of the Global Alliance in the future (next Summit 2007 Japan).

Internationally we are a member of the Global Alliance of Ministries for Peace/Departments of Peace working towards the creation of Ministries for Peace/Departments of Peace in all governments so that national ministers may meet on a regular basis, especially during crises with a mandate for conflict prevention and an ongoing emphasis on reaching peace by peaceful means through studying the root causes of the conflict. The aims of the Global Alliance is to call upon governments of the world and civil societies everywhere to:

- Develop necessary resources and infrastructures for resolving/transforming conflicts effectively by peaceful means.
- Establish, train and develop civil peace-building services.
- Incorporate conflict transformation and peace-building skills into school curricula from primary schools through university.
- Actively engage youth, women and communities to participate as equals in peace-building to ensure participation and representation of all.
- Support and encourage coordinated efforts to gather lessons

learned and best practice from peace building experience around the world.

This worldwide campaign to establish Ministries for Peace/Departments of Peace in governments everywhere is gathering momentum. This is not surprising as there is a growing realisation that at the highest level of decision-making the voice of the peacemakers must be heard, must be professionalized and institutionalized and given equal attention to every other concern.

In order to carry out our programme we would welcome people to come forward to join our working group, we are currently in need of people with peace-building skills but all those who feel a strong desire to help take initiative forward are equally welcome. Everyone has something important to contribute.

We would also like to invite you to send your news for our website, or create a link to your organization's website to binnie.innocenti@ministeroperlapaceitalia.org.

Source: Ministero per la Pace, Italia, ministeroperlapaceitalia.org/proposed-mandate

Proposed Ministers Mandate

A Ministry for Peace for Italy to Implement a Culture of Peace

Drawing inspiration from the Ministry for Peace initiatives in Australia, Canada, UK, Japan and [the] US, the proposed Minister would hold PEACE as an organizing principle in our society and we would identify the following objectives as being part of the Minister's mandate:

1 Promote the role of Italy as a European and Global Peacemaker/Peacebuilder developing new approaches to conflict prevention and the transformation of conflicts by peaceful means, at home and abroad.

2 Foster a Culture of Peace through education at all levels of

school/university and society in general by introducing training programmes in creating DIALOGUE, conflict prevention and conflict transformation skills.

3   Promote RESPECT for all human rights by distributing the Universal Declaration of Human Rights at all levels of society – which includes access to clean water – and fully implementing international instruments on human rights.

4   Ensure equality between men and women in social, economic and political decision making. Eliminate all forms of violence against women in crisis situations resulting from war and other forms of violence at home and in society.

5   Ensure greater involvement of Women in Peace, Security Conflict Prevention and Transformation (UNSCR 1325).

6   Promote international peace through actions such as the promotion of HUMAN SECURITY, the promotion of disarmament and the strengthening of non-military means of peace-making.

7   Promote dialogue among civilizations, actions in favour of vulnerable groups, immigrants, refugees, displaced persons, stateless people and traditional groups. Promoting respect for religious and cultural diversity.

8   Target the eradication of poverty, focusing on the special needs of women and children, working towards environmental sustainability, fostering national and international co-operation to reduce economic and social inequalities.

9   Facilitate the development of peace and reconciliation initiatives and encourage the development of peace-building programmes in local communities.

10 Support for independent media in the promotion of a culture of peace, create measures to address the reporting of violence in the media, share knowledge and information through new technologies.

Given the recent escalation of conflict at home, in the media, in politics and across the world today, we are convinced that this is an idea whose time has come and we are committed to carrying this project forward together with our international colleagues everywhere.

Source: Ministero per la Pace, Italia ministeroperlapaceitalia.org/proposed-mandate

The Canadian Peace Initiative for Establishment of a Department of Peace within the Government of Canada, 2011

Given the escalation of violent conflict, nuclear threat, and lawlessness across our shared globe today, there has never been greater urgency or a better window of opportunity to promote the Canadian Peace Initiative.

The Canadian Peace Initiative (CPI) is committed to the establishment of a Department of Peace within the Government of Canada. The Department of Peace would work towards building a new architecture of peace by establishing and supporting a culture of peace and assertive non-violence in Canada and the world.

We are part of a growing international movement that includes citizens from some 50 countries represented in the Global Alliance for Ministries and Infrastructures of Peace. Four governments have already established Ministers of Peace: the Solomon Islands (2005), Nepal (2007), Costa Rica (2009), and most recently the Autonomous Region of Bougainville, Papua New Guinea.

Our initiative has chapters and contacts across Canada and is endorsed by more than 30 national organizations and eminent individuals. Supporters of the CPI include such prominent Canadians as the Honourable Lloyd Axworthy and Senators Doug Roche and Dr Anne Pearson. The CPI is also supported by several organizations that together represent two million Canadians, such as the Council of Canadians, the World Federalist Movement-Canada, and Physicians for Global Survival.

Our strategy is to use Bill C-373, An Act to Establish the Department of Peace, as a road map and build a groundswell of support among the Canadian people, to make the idea compelling to politicians.

The proposed mandate:

1 **Develop early detection and rapid response processes** to deal with emerging conflicts and establish systemic responses to post-conflict demobilization, reconciliation and reconstruction.

2 **Lead internationally** to abolish nuclear, biological and chemical weapons; to reduce conventional weapon arsenals; and to ban the weaponization of space.

3 **Implement the 1999 UN Declaration** and Programme of Action on a Culture of Peace to safeguard human rights and enhance the security of persons and their communities.

4 **Implement UN Resolution 1325** to protect and support the key role played by women in the wide spectrum of peace-building work.

5 **Establish a Civilian Peace Service** that, with other training organizations, will recruit, train, and accredit peace professionals and volunteers to work at home and abroad, as an alternative to armed intervention.

6 **Address issues of violence in Canada** by promoting non-violent approaches that encourage community involvement and responsibility, such as Restorative Justice, Non-violent Communication, and Alternate Dispute Resolution.

7 **Support the development of peace education** at all levels, including post-secondary peace and conflict studies.

8 **Promote the transition** from a war-based to a peace-based economy.

9 **Establish processes of reconciliation** with Canada's indigenous peoples.

Source: Canada Peace Initiative,
canadianpeaceinitiative.ca/learn

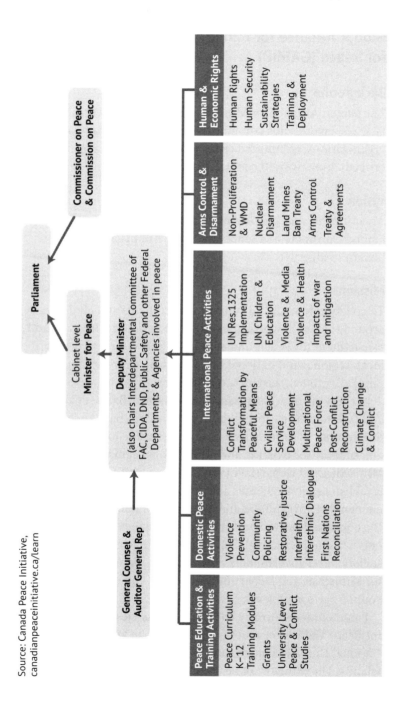

Global Alliance for Ministries and Infrastructures for Peace (GAMIP)

Background

The Global Alliance for Ministries and Infrastructures for Peace is a worldwide community of civil society campaigns, organizations, committed citizens, and appointed government officials from over 50 countries (so far).

Vision

A world where all people, individually and collectively, embody, promote and practice a culture of peace for the benefit of all.

Mission

To collaborate with and support governments and civil society around the world working to establish national ministries and Department for Peace, and also to support efforts to develop local, regional and national peace council, peace academies [and] effective infrastructures for peace.

In carrying out this mission, the Global Alliance enables and facilitates the capacity of its network to share and provide one another with resources, information, encouragement and support for existing and new national campaigns for Ministries and Departments for Peace as well as efforts to establish peace academies and other peace infrastructure elements in government and civil society. It also seeks through the combined activities of the Global Alliance and its broader networks, to increase global understanding amongst civil societies and governments around the world of the need for Ministries and Departments of Peace and civil society counterparts at all levels.

Four countries already have such ministries: The Ministry for Peace and Reconstruction in Nepal; The Ministry of National Unity, Reconciliation and Peace in the Solomon Islands; The Ministry of Peace and Justice in Costa Rica;

and the Ministry of Peace and CPA Implementation in South
Sudan. Other countries, such as Kenya and Ghana, have other
forms of Peace Infrastructures at all levels, from the local to
the national. And many countries have academies of peace
and similar organizations in educating for a culture of peace
including: Canada, Costa Rica, Nepal, Romania, Rwanda,
Switzerland, [the US] and others.

Global Summits for Ministries and Infrastructures of Peace

A principal activity of the Global Alliance is its support for the
biennial Global Summits for Ministries and Infrastructures of
Peace. The principal aims of the Global Summits are to build
relationships, share experiences, learn from one another, have
trainings that expand the bank of knowledge and scales of the
community and raise awareness of the movement in the eyes
of governments and the civil society.

The first Global Summit attended by delegates of a dozen
countries was held in October 2005 in the [UK], where the
decision to form the Global Alliance was made. The second
was held in June 2006 in Canada, the third in Japan in
September 2007 and over 100 people from over 22 countries
attended the fourth summit in Costa Rica in September 2009.
The fifth Global Summit was held in Cape Town, South Africa
in October 2011 and the sixth Global Summit in Geneva,
Switzerland in September 2013. The seventh summit is in
Lagos, Nigeria in November 2015.

Among the key outcomes of the past summits are an
associated global youth movement, the African Alliance for
Ministries and Infrastructures for Peace, and the successful
establishment of the Ministry of Justice and Peace in Costa
Rica and the Ministry of Peace and Reconstruction in Nepal.

Principles of the Global Alliance for Ministries and Infrastructures for Peace

As we continue our journey to govern ourselves in a culture
of peace, we acknowledge that, in order to fulfil our vision

and mission, we must live and practice a culture of peace. Therefore, we recognize that it is essential that our work be grounded in and reflect such healthy relationships as goodwill, non-violence, cooperation, harmlessness, clarity, simplicity, interconnectedness, inclusivity, understanding, honest communications, living a culture of peace, shared responsibility and shared leadership.

Address:
Chemin De La Caracole
68/CH
1294
Genthod
Geneva
Switzerland

Website: www.gamip.org
Email: info@gamip.org
Telephone: +41(01)225357370 or 234-8026659958

Source: GAMIP, gamip.org/about.html

The Minister for Peace and Disarmament: An Assessment – Conscience UK (2018)

By Dr Tim Street

Introduction

This report provides an assessment of the Labour Party's proposal to create a Minister for Peace and Disarmament (MPD) and highlights the political and practical obstacles to, and opportunities for, the post being a success. Conducting this assessment was important, firstly because of the lack of civil society and public discussion concerning what the remit and implications of an MPD would be. Secondly, the controversial nature of several of the issues that the MPD could cover, such as regulating the arms trade or conventional and nuclear disarmament, require careful consideration if appropriate policy proposals are to be developed.

Overall, based on the responses of people from the peace, disarmament and security community interviewed for this study, the relevant institutional experiences of British and foreign governments and the current state of domestic and international politics, the report concludes that there is significant potential in the MPD concept, but that it requires further thought and attention from Labour and civil society before it is established and developed in government.

1.1 The roots of the MPD – precedents and potential for success:

- The UK has substantial institutional experience on matters of arms control, non-proliferation and disarmament. This includes having a Minister for Disarmament under a Labour government in the 1960s. Such posts function optimally when the government involved makes these issues a priority and good relations exist amongst the world's major powers.
- Current multilateral nuclear non-proliferation and disarmament efforts involving the UK are at a standstill,

with the Conservative government showing little or no interest in the subject, whilst relations between Russia and the USA are at a low point. This situation clearly presents significant obstacles to the MPD's agenda, but opportunities to show leadership also exist.

- The idea of an MPD has roots in, and would complement various initiatives by, the UN and other international bodies. For example, the UN's agenda for Human Security and Sustaining Peace could be advanced by the MPD.

- One means of developing the MPD concept would be to learn from the experiences of other countries. For example, recent research shows that dominant national narratives may strongly determine policy outcomes, perpetuating continuity and blocking progressive reform on international policy.

- If the MPD is to have a lasting impact, a Labour government would thus need to find a way of reorienting the UK's wider approach to national and international security policy in a progressive direction.

1.2 The international context – what does 'Global Britain' mean for the MPD?:

- The Conservative government's post-Brexit vision of 'Global Britain' focuses on military power projection and the development of relationships with authoritarian regimes. In contrast, Labour has committed to an ethical foreign policy, focusing on human rights, democracy, diplomacy and peace building.

- Despite this, and Jeremy Corbyn's willingness to challenge the status quo in these areas, Labour's recent approach to defence and foreign policy has been relatively cautious and moderate.

- Historically, proposals to substantively redirect the UK's international policy in a progressive direction have faced strong domestic resistance from economic, military and political elites, with British dependence on the [US] presenting a significant obstacle internationally.

- Given the gap between what the public and decision-making elites think should be the priorities for national security, an opportunity exists for Labour to present a new approach that reflects public concerns and explains, for example, how an ethical foreign policy led by the MPD can reduce terrorism.

- An opportunity also exists for Labour and the MPD to address the highly secretive nature of international policy and prioritize transparency, democracy and accountability on these issues in government.

- More ambitious changes to the UK's international policy will require an active civil society working alongside the MPD and sympathetic political parties to alter popular conceptions of security, provide education and harness support for progressive action, for example, on nuclear disarmament.

1.3 The domestic context – can Labour forge a new consensus on UK defence and foreign policy?:

- Developing a consensus on a new direction for UK international policy is complicated by the fact that whilst the UK public may be war weary following the invasions of Iraq and Afghanistan, a lingering sense of national greatness and nostalgia for empire remains in their 'deep story' concerning British identity.

- Ongoing internal conflict in Labour, the relatively low electoral salience of defence and foreign policy, the Conservative party's 'ownership' of the defence debate and public distrust concerning Labour's competency on national security are also barriers to developing progressive approaches to security.

- Labour's task is therefore to understand the 'deep story' of the British people and propose a positive alternative vision for the UK's international policy which responds to their hopes, fears, beliefs, needs and interests.

- The MPD could ensure that the 'Global Britain' concept focuses on diplomacy and peace-making, for which there is significant public support. Whilst such measures will help implement an ethical foreign policy in the short-term, advancing national and international nuclear non-proliferation and disarmament will require longer-term efforts by the MPD and civil society.
- Although the Conservative Party is clearly opposed to the MPD concept, support would likely be forthcoming – to different degrees – from the Greens, Liberal Democrats, Plaid Cymru and Scottish National Party.

2.1 The potential strengths and weaknesses of an MPD:

The interviews conducted with the peace, disarmament and security community for this report provided several relevant findings regarding the potential strengths and weaknesses of Labour's MPD proposal.

1. In terms of arguments for or potential strengths of the MPD, these included:
2. Institutionalizing support for peace, diplomacy and international law
3. Contributing to peace and disarmament education
4. Promoting alternative approaches to security such as non-offensive defence
5. Linking up peace and disarmament with environmental and social justice
6. Developing the UK's conflict resolution and peace building work
7. Realizing arms conversion and defence diversification / reducing military spending
8. Advancing nuclear disarmament and the nuclear ban treaty
9. Ensuring the participation of women and a gendered perspective in policymaking
10. Engaging with civil society at home and abroad
11. Diverting tax contributions to support non-violent approaches to security

In terms of arguments against and potential weaknesses of the MPD, these included:

The danger of the MPD being 'window dressing'

1. Lack of an international partner or disarmament workplan / tensions with Russia
2. Previous problems with posts similar to the MPD
3. Duplicating existing work of other departments / money better spent elsewhere
4. The problematic 'peace and disarmament' title
5. Lack of public support or awareness / media opposition
6. The role being too narrow or weak

2.2 Situating the MPD in its institutional context:

- Labour currently propose that the MPD post will involve a hub and spokes arrangement to implement their, as yet unpublished, 'peace doctrine'. It is also envisaged that the MPD will be based out of a small private office operating at cabinet level.

- These arrangements appear to correspond well with the role as envisaged by several interviewees, who highlighted the need for the MPD to have a monitoring and oversight role in relation to other departments. Some argued that this would ensure that reforms pursuant to an ethical foreign policy were implemented.

- However, in order to avoid the MPD becoming disempowered or marginalized in office, the post would need to have the Prime Minister's backing and be part of a broader reconsideration of UK defence and foreign policy which had significant support from civil society and the public.

- Regarding the allocation of resources, different options exist in relation to the size and scope of the MPD's eventual remit. Labour should be clear about its relevant departmental spending plans and how the MPD's work may be funded, for example, by providing appropriate resources from the FCO and/or Ministry of Defence (MOD).

2.3 Five options for the MPD:

The MPD post could be configured in several different ways. The five options presented below, which are not necessarily mutually exclusive, take the form of general approaches or characters that the post could assume:

1. New thinking to develop long-term, sustainable and human security objectives

A focus on human security, peace and disarmament could be combined with environmental and social justice in the UK's international policy, with these ideas brought into cabinet discussions by the MPD.

2. Demilitarization and disarmament

In addition to a focus on conventional and nuclear non-proliferation and disarmament, action on demilitarization led by the MPD could include: exploring non-offensive defence and a humanitarian role for the armed forces; limiting arms exports and diversifying away from the production and export of military technology as part of a transition to a green economy.

3. Diplomacy, peace building and 'soft power'

The MPD could focus on boosting international diplomatic processes such as the global nuclear ban treaty alongside other multilateral agreements and fora. Conflict resolution, prevention and peace building should also be a priority so that the UK becomes a world leader on these issues, with gender equality and rights a central focus.

4. Democratization and education

The MPD could help to develop a War Powers Act, and generally ensure that government decision-making on war and peace is opened up to wider consultation and participation. Education and outreach to the public and civil society could also prove to be an important aspect of the MPD's work.

5. Becoming an ethical foreign policy watchdog

The MPD could take on a watchdog role whereby it provided

monitoring and oversight of government departments, such as the Department for Business, Energy and Industrial Strategy, the Foreign and Commonwealth Office, the Ministry of Defence and the Department For International Development, so that they adhere to an ethical foreign policy.

3. Recommendations for Labour:

- **Ensure coherence between the title, remit and configuration of the post**
  It is important that the title of the post both appropriately reflects what work is principally to be carried out and provides clarity and coherence in relation to its aims and objectives, not least so that the Minister is provided with appropriate and justifiable resources.

- **Lead the debate on a positive alternative vision for UK international policy**
  Labour must continue to hold the government to account so that the UK acts responsibly and in line with its international legal and moral obligations. Winning the contest of ideas in opposition will, in the long-term, enable Labour to be more ambitious if it achieves power, opening up new opportunities for the peace, disarmament and human security agenda.

For the Shadow MPD:

- **Be visible, direct, open to engagement and able to deal with criticism**
  Several actions could be taken to develop the MPD role in opposition. For example, Labour should consult with academia, civil society and other military and security experts regarding the 'peace doctrine' prior to its publication, and ideas such as a humanitarian-focused military, new Peace, Disarmament and Security Select Committee and UK-Nordic Council on human security explored.

- **Hold the government to account and build parliamentary support for reform**

Opportunities to be a champion of an ethical foreign policy in opposition include: advocating for the establishment of a War Powers Act; making the case for a critical and selective partnership with the [US]; developing policy proposals for defence diversification and arms export controls; exploring how the UK may establish a progressive bloc within NATO.

For civil society:

- **Engage with Labour and other political parties on the MPD project**
  Groups involved in issues covered by the MPD should consult with Labour and other supportive parties to exchange ideas and develop shared understandings on key subjects in order to develop thinking about the post.
- **Build cooperation and develop shared strategies**
  Such groups should also convene joint meetings to discuss areas of mutual agreement to help advance, inform and create public discussion about the MPD's future work.

Written by Dr Tim Street. Published by Conscience: Taxes for Peace Not War.
URL: www.ConscienceOnline.org.uk
Full report: www.conscienceonline.org.uk/mpdrep

United Nations General Assembly Draft Resolution: Building 'Ministries or Departments of Peace' within Governments to Strengthen the Culture of Peace

DRAFT RESOLUTION (rev. 4/26/10)

Building 'infrastructures of peace' within governments to strengthen the culture of peace
The General Assembly,

Guided by all the United Nations (UN) documents written on the Culture of Peace since June, 1945, in particular the **Charter of the United Nations**, dedicated to saving succeeding generations from the scourge of war, its call for nations to live together in peace as good neighbours, and taking to heart its emphasis on the vital role 'We the Peoples of the United Nations' are to play in 'realizing a peaceful, just and compassionate neighbourhood,'

Reaffirming the **Universal Declaration of Human Rights** that the foundation of freedom, justice and peace is recognition of the inherent rights of all members of the human family, and that all human beings should act towards one another peacefully,

Recalling its resolution 52/15 of 20 November 1997, proclaiming the year 2000 as the '**International Year for the Culture of Peace**', and A/RES/53/25 of 19 November 1998, proclaiming 2001-2010 the "**International Decade for a Culture of Peace and Nonviolence for the Children of the World**,'

Emphasizing its resolution 53/243 of 6 October 1999, in which the **UN Declaration and Programme of Action for a Culture of Peace** gives clear guidelines for governments, non-governmental organizations (NGOs) and civil society – people within all walks of life -- to work together to strengthen the Culture of Peace as we enter the second decade of the 21st century,

Remembering the **Constitution of the UN Educational, Scientific and Cultural Organization** (UNESCO), which states that '*since wars begin in the minds of men [sic], it is in the minds of men [sic] that the defences of peace must be constructed*' and the important role UNESCO is mandated to play promoting the Culture of Peace,

Recalling the many other key UN Culture of Peace documents including:
- A/RES/52/13, 15 January 1998 Culture of Peace;
- A/RES/55/282, 28 September 2001 International Day of Peace;
- 2005 Mid-Decade Status Report on the International Decade for a Culture of Peace and Nonviolence for the Children of the World,

Reaffirming Security Council resolutions 1325 of 31 October 2001 on **Women, Peace and Security,** which acknowledges for the first time the crucial importance of women's participation in the peace processes, and follow-up Security Council Resolution 1820 of 19 June 2008 by same name,

Standing in solidarity with all efforts to overcome the persistence of conflict in various parts of the world and proliferation of nuclear weapons, which threaten the existence of our planet,

Distressed that men, women and children in their billions have suffered the atrocities of war, poverty and human-induced environmental disasters, now more than ever is committed to saving future generations from the scourge of war, determined to live in peace and to build the Culture of Peace at the individual, national and global levels,

Believing in the goodwill of all the Member States of the UN and in the increasing political will of each Member State to 'promote social progress and better standards of life in larger freedom,'

Acknowledging the urgent need to re-build trust of people in governments and establish effective working relationships between governments and their citizens - in the spirit of cooperation for the common good,

Aware of the increasingly significant role the **Economic and Social Council** will play,

Encouraged by the work of the **UN Peacebuilding Commission** with its mandate to bring together all relevant actors, including NGOs and civil society, in joint efforts to assist countries emerging from conflict to achieve sustainable peace,

Endorsing the view expressed in the **Security Council's Presidential Statement** (document S/PRST/2005/42) of the potentially vital contribution that a vibrant and diverse civil society can make towards reconciliation and peace-building between conflicting communities,

Cognizant of the UN mandated **Global Partnership for the Prevention of Armed Conflict** December, 2007 Issue Paper entitled 'Joint Action for Prevention: Civil Society and Government Cooperation on Conflict Prevention and Peace-building,' in Chapter 5 on *National Infrastructure for Responding to Conflict* (page 59) -- Why a Ministry or Department of Peace within national governments?:

- *To create peace as a primary organizing principle in society, both domestically and globally;*
- *To direct government policy towards non-violent resolution of conflict prior to escalation to violence and to seek peace by peaceful means in all conflict areas;*
- *To promote justice and democratic principles to expand human rights and the security of persons and their communities, consistent with the Universal Declaration of Human Rights, other related UN treaties and conventions, and the Declaration and Programme of Action on a Culture of Peace (1999);*
- *To promote disarmament and develop and strengthen non-military options of peace-making and peace-building;*

- *To develop new approaches to non-violent intervention, and utilize constructive dialogue, mediation and the peaceful resolution of conflict at home and abroad;*
- *To encourage the involvement in local, national, and global peace-building of local communities, faith groups, NGOs, and other civil society and business organizations, including the formation of civilian non-violent peace forces;*
- *To facilitate the development of peace and reconciliation summits to promote non-violent communication and mutually beneficial solutions;*
- *To act as a resource for the creation and the gathering of best practices documents, lessons learned, and peace impact assessment;*
- *To provide for the training of all military and civilian personnel who administer post-war reconstruction and demobilization in war-torn societies; and*
- *To fund the development of peace education curriculum materials for use at all educational levels and to support university-level peace studies.*
  1. *Urges* the Secretary-General to actively encourage all UN Member States to build the Culture of Peace architecture nationally – and in collaboration with the community of nations – by creating structures across national governments to direct policies and programmes in peace-building; and that these structures be in the form of *Ministries or Departments of Peace*, to support fulfilment of the vision in the UN Declaration and Programme of Action for a Culture of Peace (1999);
  2. *Invites* the Secretary-General to create a link within the UN system to facilitate coordination with the national *Ministries or Departments of Peace*, in collaborative efforts to promote the Culture of Peace. {Such link would evaluate how all adopted UN actions contribute to the Culture of Peace by having Culture of Peace 'Impact Assessments'.};
  3. *Requests* that the Secretary General refer to the *UN*

Advisory Committee on Administrative and Budgetary Questions the idea of setting up a Voluntary Fund to allocate resources for addressing these essential peace-building activities that protect through prevention; to begin the 'economic conversion' shift from military to civilian production, so as to 'beat our swords into ploughshares and spears into pruning hooks;'

4. *Reaffirms* its pledge, as representatives of the governments of the world, to join 'We the Peoples' in building a peaceful world, in the spirit of the UN Charter; advancing the Culture of Peace within each nation, each culture, each religion, and each human being.

Source: Peace Through Unity, peacethroughunity.info/downloads/ UNResolutionrevsept9.doc

Index